This book is copyright. Except for the purpose of fair review, no part may be stored or transmitted in any form or by any means, electronic or mechanical, including recording or storage in any information retrieval system, without permission in writing from the publisher and author. No reproduction may be made, whether by scanning, photocopying, or by any other means, unless a license has been obtained from the publisher and author or their agent.

© Copyright 2013 by C. Neil Linton

All rights reserved.

ISBN-13: 978-0-4732-6707-0

ISBN-10: 0-4732-6707-1

(LCCN) Library of Congress Catalog Card No. 00-000000

Published by CenterLine®, Auckland, New Zealand

Cover's Digital Design by: C. Neil Linton

Cover image background - licensed via depositphotos.com
(Assorted Magnetic Words by THPStock, Australia)

Printed in The United States of America (U.S.A.)

10 9 8 7 6 5 4 3 2 1

~ Dedicated to my mother **Shirley Ann Messer-Linton** *~*

I acknowledge and appreciate my life, for all that it is, and to those that stand beside me in support of it.

I aspire to forgive others and myself, freely accepting that every human being strives to do their best with the knowledge, experience, and vigor that they possess today. I strive to accept others for who they are, and where they are in their personal growth.

Total enlightenment or perfection is a destination seen on our horizon that we conceptualize and then endeavor to progress toward, overcoming challenges and disappointments --- driven by hope.

Each moment the universe unfolds countless treasures to be admired and cherished. Have eyes wide-open to observe and experience the many miracles that surround us.

Be present in the moment, have gratitude and give freely of yourself to others, absent of expectation. Treasure each day that affords you.

C.L.

A Student's Study Guide of English Language Grammar, Punctuation, and Writing

- First Edition

A Simple, Easy to Understand Reference and Guide for English as a Second or Foreign Language Students

Written By: **C. Neil Linton** - MEdLead, TESOL
Author, Educator, and English Language Facilitator.

Contributing Editors: **L'Shawn Howard** - M.A. (TESOL)
Miho Yatabori - (TESOL)

The Eight (8) Parts of Speech in Simple Terms

English Language Punctuation

A Writing Guide

Practice Dialogs and Role-plays

Irregular Verb Chart

Abbreviations Common of English Words or Phrases

English Language Pronunciation Chart

(International Phonetic Alphabet)

QUOTE:

"What words say does not last. The words last, because words are always the same, and what they say is never the same."

Antonio Porchia, Voces (1943):
Translated from Spanish by W.S. Merwin

ACKNOWLEDGEMENTS

During the manuscript stage, *A Student's Study Guide of English Language Grammar, Punctuation, and Writing* was influenced greatly from the valuable feedback received from passionate teachers, experienced English language specialists and countless dedicated students from around the world, who are, or have been, studying English as a Second or Foreign Language (ESL / EFL). Any and all feedback is priceless. Those that have a passion to seek ongoing personal and professional development can only see such feedback as an opportunity for improvement.

I'd like to thank the following individuals who have given selfless support and encouragement by imparting valuable knowledge and wisdom, answering professional questions related to English language grammar, punctuation, writing, or the publishing industry, all collectively and immeasurably contributing, directly or indirectly, to this comprehensive collection:

David Hopkins, English Language Instructor and Lead Teacher for Self-Learning at King Saud University, Saudi Arabia, who had inspired me toward becoming a confident professional English language teacher; **Marc Helgesen**, ESL / ELT Author, Professor at Miyagi Gakuin Women's University, Sendai, Japan and Adjunct Professor at the Teachers College, Columbia University Master of Arts (MA) Teaching English to Speakers of Other Languages (TESOL) Program – Tokyo; **David Paul**, ESL / ELT Author and President at Language Teaching Professionals; **Andrew Gibbons** (Mentor), Senior Lecturer at Auckland University of Technology (AUT), New Zealand; **Robert Murphy**, Lecturer at The University of Kitakyushu; **Chuck Sandy** and **Curtis Kelly**, ELT materials writers and teachers; **Steven Nishida**, Director at Nara Institute of Science and Technology; **Ryan Hagglund**, Adjunct Professor at Yamagata University and President / CEO of My English Schools, Yamagata, Japan; **Paul Price**, President of Nine-Point-Nine English Schools, Yamagata, Japan; **and Michael Wyatt**, Language Coordinator at Al Sharjah, Ash Shāriqah, United Arab Emirates (U.A.E.).

My gratitude also goes to: **John King**, Founding Partner & CEO at Cultural Architecture; **Dave Logan**, Faculty Member at Marshall School of Business; **Kadambari Gladding**, TV Presenter / Director / Reporter; **Deborah Sandella**, Award-winning Author, International Speaker and originator of the R.I.M. Method at The RIM Institute, and an Associate at Jack Canfield Companies; **Sharon McGloin**, President / Owner at Experiential Alternatives, and Adjunct Professor at Avila University; **Richard Lin**, Director of the MindFirst Academy, International Meta-NLP Academy, and the International MindMap Academy; **Scott Schilling**, Owner, Schilling Sales & Marketing, Inc.; **Shawn Wiesner**, Change Agent at the Wiser Group Inc.; **Celine Egan**, Co-owner at the Direct Selling Entrepreneurs Network; **Beau Henderson**, Founder & CEO of RichLife Advisors; **Geoff Nicholson**, Founder of GN-Coaching: Stress and Empowerment Experts; **Ike Parker**, Founder / Facilitator at Brooksong Center; **Miho Yatabori**, Contributing Editor; **Norry Ascroft**; **Lloyd & Christine Hollis**, Entrepreneurs; **Tanya Davis**, The University of California, San Diego; **Wayne Miller**, Teacher & Musician; **Jacob Gwynn**, Independent Creative Professional; **Janna Androutsou**, English Language Specialist, ESL Teacher and TESOL Teacher Trainer; **Dongxue** (Sammi) **Yan**, Chartered Public Accountant (C.P.A); and **Lynn Tashima**.

Special thanks to my wonderful parents **Gerald W. and Shirley A. Linton**. Also to: **Kelvyn** and **Krystal**; **Thomas**, **Carrie** and **William**; **David**, **Gavyn**, **Meegan**, and **Robson**, who have all positively touched my life.

PERSONAL ENDORSEMENTS

My sincere gratitude goes to the following gifted individuals who have personally endorsed my life's work:

Firstly, to the one-and-only **Jack Canfield**, *America's #1 Success Coach* and a best selling author of *Chicken Soup for the Soul* book series, *The Success Principals: How to get from where you are to where you want to be,* and a teacher in *'The Secret'*.

It has been Jack's indirect and personal face-to-face mentorship, which started back in October 2009, in San Diego, California, that has inspired me to actively and passionately create, believe-in, and pursue my goals.

"I have a great deal of love in my heart for you, your chosen mission, and the work you have done and are doing in the world."

Jack Canfield

"C. Neil Linton is a man with tremendous heart. His compassion for humanity has lead him to his life's work and it is apparent upon first meeting him that he is convicted in his purpose. His insatiable thirst to learn becomes your asset once you choose to work with him and he has studied with the best of the best. If you seek a successful, driven, compassionate individual, look no further."

Erin Tullius

Human Potential and Wellness Practitioner

"C. Neil Linton not only 'talks the talk' but what is more important is he 'walks the walk.' His determination to live out genuine life change has inspired me greatly. I'm grateful for his example, friendship and work."

Mike Pate
Executive Director, Transformation Ministries

"C. Neil Linton has taken the lessons of the masters and mentors and made them his own. He has a captivating way of bringing information to life, helping others to put it into action, to move forward towards their greatest potential."

Scott Schilling
Personal Trainer, Speaker, Author and Philanthropist

CONTENTS

ACKNOWLEDGMENTS	VII
PERSONAL ENDORSEMENTS	IX
INTRODUCTION	IXX
CHAPTER ONE: ENGLISH WORDS	
EIGHT (8) PARTS OF SPEECH	1
PART ONE — Nouns (n.)	1
Proper Nouns	3
Common Nouns	4
Singular and Plural Nouns	4
Countable Nouns	5
Uncountable Nouns	5
Collective Nouns	6
Concrete Nouns	6
Abstract Nouns	6
Possessive Nouns	7
Determiners (det.)	8
Articles	10
Indefinite – *'a'* and *'an'*	10
Definite – *'the'*	11
General Article Rules	12
Zero Articles (Zero Determiners)	12
Demonstratives	14
Possessives	14
Quantifiers	15
Numbers and Ordinals	16
There Is a Correct Way to Write Numbers	16
Pre-determiners	16

PART TWO — Adjectives (adj.)	17
Adjectives Before Nouns or After Verbs	18
Comparative and Superlative Adjectives	19
One-syllable Adjectives	19
Two-syllable Adjectives	20
Adjectives of Three or More Syllables	21
Irregular Adjectives	21
Meaning Differences with Adjectives	22
Correct Adjective Order	22
PART THREE — Pronouns (pron.)	24
Personal Pronouns	24
First, Second or Third-Person	25
Demonstrative Pronouns	26
Relative Pronouns	28
Interrogative Pronouns	29
Indefinite Pronouns	30
Negative Pronouns	31
Reciprocal Pronouns	31
PART FOUR — Verbs (v.)	32
Main (Principal) Verbs	32
Active and Passive Voice	32
Auxiliary Verbs	34
Primary Auxiliary Verbs (be, do, have)	35
Primary Auxiliary Verb 'be' and Its Forms	35
Primary Auxiliary Verb 'do' and Its Forms	38
Primary Auxiliary Verb 'have' and Its Forms	39
Modal Auxiliary Verbs	41
Regular and Irregular Verbs	45
Verb Tense and Future Time	46
Present Simple	47
Past Simple	49
Future Simple	50
Present Continuous	51
Past Continuous	52
Future Continuous	54

Present Perfect	56
Past Perfect	58
Future Perfect	59
Present Perfect Continuous	60
Past Perfect Continuous	62
Future Perfect Continuous	63
Subject Verb Agreement	64
Anyone, Everyone, Someone...	64
Together with, As well as, Along with	65
Neither and Either	65
Nor or Or	66
There and Here	66
Verbs in the Present Tense	66
Nouns Ending with 's'	66
Fractional Expressions	66
Positive Verses Negative Subject	67
PART FIVE — Adverbs (adv.)	68
Adverb Use	68
Adverb Types	68
Other Uses	70
Adverb Intensifiers	70
Forming an Adverb	71
Adverb Placement	72
Adverb Order	72
Conjunctive Adverbs	73
Interrogative Adverbs	74
PART SIX — Prepositions (prep.)	75
Place, Space & Direction (at, in, on, ...)	77
Time (at, in, on, ...)	78
Compound or Complex Prepositions	79
PART SEVEN — Conjunctions (conj.)	80
Coordinating Conjunctions	80
Subordinating Conjunctions	81
Correlative or Double Conjunctions	82
PART EIGHT — Interjections (interj.)	84

CHAPTER TWO: PUNCTUATION GUIDE

ENGLISH LANGUAGE PUNCTUATION — 85
ACCEPTABLE USAGE — 85
Terminating Marks (.) (!) (?) (‽) — 85
- Period or Full Stop (.) — 85
- Exclamation Mark (!) — 86
- Question Mark (?) — 86
- Interrobang (‽) — 87

Ellipsis (...) — 87
Comma (,) — 88
- Distinguishing Parenthetical Elements — 88
- Separating Items in a Series — 89
- Serial (Oxford or Harvard) Comma — 89
- Introductory Phrase or Adverb Clause — 89
- Setting Off Interruptions — 90
- Separating Dialog and Non-dialog Text — 90
- Before a Coordinating Conjunction — 91
- Separating Date Elements — 91
- Separating Number Elements — 92
- Within Names, Places, and Addresses — 93

Colon (:) — 93
Semicolon (;) — 94
Dash (—) or (--), and Swung Dash (~) — 95
Hyphen (-) — 96
- Between Compound Words — 96
- Two Words Linked by a Preposition — 96
- Spelt Numbers and Cardinal — 96
- Words with a Prefix — 97
- Words with a Suffix — 98

Apostrophe (') — 99
- Omission of Letters in a Contraction — 99
- With Possessive Nouns — 99

Parentheses ( ) and Brackets [ ] — 99
- Parentheses ( ) — 99
- Brackets [ ] — 101

Double and Single Quotation Marks (" ") (' ')	102
Capital Letters (Aa Bb Cc)	102
Inconspicuous Stressing: Italics	104
Bolding	105
Bullet Points	106

CHAPTER THREE: WRITING GUIDE

THE WRITING PROCESS	107
COMPOSITION and ACADEMIC WRITING	107
Prewriting: Organizing Thoughts	107
Mind Mapping	108
Spider Diagram	109
Bubble Map	110
Drafting	110
Paragraph Construction	111
Topic Sentence	111
Supporting Sentences	111
Concluding Sentences	112
Sentence Unity and Coherence	112
Misused Words	114
Homonym, Homograph, Homophone	114
Composition, Essay, or Article	117
Transitional Sentence	117
Revising and Editing	118
Proofing	119
Submitting or Publishing	119
Submitting	119
Publishing	119

APPENDIX – STUDENT RESOURCES   121

Dialogs and Role-plays	121
List of Irregular Verbs	125
Abbreviations Common of English Words	133
English Language Pronunciation Chart	
(International Phonetic Alphabet)	137

INDEX   139

INTRODUCTION

*W*ho might benefit from *A Student's Study* Guide of *English Language Grammar, Punctuation and Writing* reference book?

A Student's Study Guide of *English Language Grammar, Punctuation and Writing* reference book has been thoughtfully created drawing on almost two-decades of knowledge and wisdom gained as an English as a Second or Foreign Language Facilitator as well as an English Language School and TESOL Teacher Training College owner.

It has been created as a comprehensive alternative to the intimidating thick and costly technical grammar books most English students accumulate. These books are often filled with linguistic academic jargon that is not easily understood by English language learners (students), not to mention being heavy to drag around.

This book will benefit and assist English language students who are:

- preparing to enter a bi-lingual society with employment and social opportunities,
- High school and University students who are enrolled in an English language course or qualification.
- Students who are planning to study abroad at an English language school in an English speaking or bi-lingual country.
- Learners who may be a little weak in English grammar and usage and require a tool that will provide the answers needed at a moments notice,
- People who may have a need for further professional development, upgrading or refreshment of the skills learnt when younger.

With an English language students' needs in mind, this book has been packed with relevant, practical examples and advice in simple easy to understand terms. It also provides an English language punctuation and writing guide to assist with constructing paragraphs, writing essays, creating business and personal letters, memos, or emails. It is also lightweight and easily carried with you for easy reference. You can't afford to be without it.

What is the purpose of *A Student's Study Guide of English Language Grammar, Punctuation, and Writing* reference book?

A Student's Study Guide of English Language Grammar, Punctuation, and Writing reference book contains six chapters and an appendix of student resources.

Chapter One is a comprehensive outline to the eight (8) parts of speech found in English language grammar and its usage, in simple terms. You will find easy to understand explanations and real-life sentence examples for each concept.

Grammar and usage of the English language is extremely complex. *A Student's Study Guide of English Language Grammar, Punctuation, and Writing* reference book was never intended to be a complete dictionary of English grammar and usage, but a comprehensive sampling for quick reference. A deeper investigation into each concept by the English language learner can be researched and knowledge improved, as needed, over time.

Chapter Two is an English language punctuation guide. The collection can be used as a reference to assist the English language student in the correct use of punctuation as they write.

Chapter Three is a writing guide for students. It provides invaluable information and guidance to all skill levels of writers who may attempt a simple composition, a more complex academic essay, or an advanced formal article. The mechanics from preparation to completion are basically the same.

How to use *A Student's Study Guide of English Language Grammar, Punctuation, and Writing* reference book?

A Student's Study Guide of English Language Grammar, Punctuation, and Writing reference book has been designed as a slightly over-sized pocket reference, intended for day-to-day use, and to be carried from class-to-class, location-to-location, by the English language student.

CHAPTER ONE: ENGLISH WORDS

EIGHT (8) PARTS OF SPEECH

PART ONE — Nouns (n.)

A *noun* is a naming word used to define a *person, place,* or *object*. A *noun* can also define an *idea, emotion* (*state*), or a *quality*. A *noun* can be recognized within a sentence by its *naming function, form,* and *position*. In most cases a *noun* can follow a *determiner*, such as:

    Articles: *a, an, the*

a **book**	an **apple**	the **people**

    Numbers: *one, two, three*

one **pencil**	two **erasers**	three **dogs**

    Ordinals: *first, second, third*

first **impression**	second **house**	third **person**

    Quantifiers: *a few, many, most, several, each, every, some, all, any*

a few **men**	many **ships**	most **students**
several **days**	each **life**	every **hour**
some **cheese**	all my **friends**	any **children**

    Possessives: *my, your, our, their, his, her, whose*

my **car**	your **office**	our **friends**
their **opinions**	his / her **happiness**	whose **ethics**

    Demonstratives: *these, those, this, that*

these / those **cats**	this **umbrella**	that **character**

A *noun* can be found before and after a verb. Examples are:

    The ***orange*** fell (v.) from the ***tree***.   The ***boy*** shut (v.) the ***door***.

A *noun* can follow either:

    Time Prepositions: *at, on, during, while, ...*

        I will visit my Mom *at **Easter**.*   I will go home *on **Friday**.*
        I enjoy skiing *during **winter**.*   It rained *while **John*** slept.

    Place Prepositions: *in, at, on, ...*

        Smoking is not allowed *in **school**.* I study Math *at **college**.*
        The Giant Sequoia tree is one of the tallest trees *on **earth**.*

Most *nouns* can have **-s** or **-es** added at the end of the word to express the *plural form* of the word. Examples are:

    *house / house**s**   church / church**es***

Most *nouns* can have an apostrophe and **-s** added to them to express *ownership* or *belonging*, called *possessive nouns*. Examples are:

    *the boy**'s** bicycles   the farmer**'s** cow   Tony**'s** car*

When a *multi-syllable plural noun* ends in **-s (es)**, then the apostrophe is placed after **-s'**. Examples are:

    *the rugby player**s'** uniforms   the lad**ies'** dresses*

However, a *one-syllable proper noun* ending in **-s** will have an apostrophe and an additional **-s** added to the word, such as:

    *Jess**'s** report*

    An exception to the above are words such as in some *names* that would be generally awkward to pronounce. An example is the name Moses:

    Moses' biblical stories

A *noun* for a specific *person, title, company, organization, place,* or *thing,* as well as their abbreviations, should have the first letter of each word capitalized. Examples are:

    Specific names: *September, Christmas, ...*
    Person: *John Lennon, Lido Anthony 'Lee' Iacocca, ...*
    Title: *Mr.* or *Mrs., Chief Executive Officer, Dean of Education, ...*
    Company: *Sony Corporation of America, Hudson's Bay Co., ...*
    Place: *Canada* or *CAN, The United Kingdom* or *U.K., ...*
    Organization: *The National Rifle Association (NRA), ...*
    Thing: *Rolls-Royce Silver Shadow, The Eiffel Tower, ...*

    An exception to this rule is when a trademark utilizes a lowercase letter for the first letter of any word within the title, such as:

    Apple's iPhone, iPad or *iPod, etc.*

Some *nouns* can be formed from adjectives by adding a suffix at the end of the adjective, such as **-ness** or **-ity**. Examples are:

    happy - *happi**ness***   responsible - *responsibi**lity***

Some *nouns* can be formed from verbs by adding a suffix at the end of the verb, such as: **-tion** or **-sion**. Examples are:

    inform - *informa**tion***   admit - *admi**ssion***

Additionally, some *nouns* can be formed from verbs and occasionally from adjectives by adding a suffix at the end of the verb or adjective, such as: **-ment**. Examples are:

    A noun from a verb: replace - *replace**ment***   enjoy - *enjoy**ment***
    A noun from an adjective: merry - *merri**ment***

Some *abstract nouns* can be formed from the original *noun* by adding a suffix at the end of that *noun*, such as: **-ship** or **-hood**. Examples are:

    neighbor**hood**   relation**ship**   friend**ship**

✼ Proper Nouns ✼

The title and / or name of a *person, place, or thing,* is usually expressed by a *proper noun* and is always capitalized. A *proper noun* can also name a *day of the week,* a *month of the year,* a *holiday* or *festival, etc.* Examples are:

    Title and / or Name of a Person: *Professor Williams, Dr. Jones, ...*
    Places: *The United States of America, Yokohama, Japan, ...*
    Regions: *North Island* of *New Zealand, Middle East, ...*
    Districts: *District of Columbia, Rochford District, ...*
    Things: *Queen Mary II (Ship), Apollo 13, ...*
    Festivals: *Cherry Blossom Festival, Maudi Graw, ...*
    Territories: *Virgin Islands, Yukon, ...*
    Provinces: *British Columbia, The Western Cape, ...*
    States: *Washington, New York, ...*
    Holidays: *Christmas, Al Hijra, ...*
    Days of the Week and Months of the Year:
        Monday through *Sunday* and *January* through *December*

Note: *Proper Nouns* do not name seasons: winter, spring, etc.

✼ Common Nouns ✼

A *common noun*, opposite to a *proper noun*, names *a general item* and is not capitalized, unless they are at the beginning of a sentence. Examples are:

    I was able to secure a job as a **professor**.
    I drove **north**, up the island for an hour.

Some examples of other *common nouns* are:

    The people you can see:

baby	boy or girl	teenager	grandparent
parent	salesclerk	police-officer	manager

    The places you can go:

house	restaurant	school	backyard
beach	river	mountain	store

    The tangible things you can see:

apple	cat	bathtub	refrigerator
camera	book	chair	window

✼ Singular and Plural Nouns ✼

Most *nouns* are either *singular* or *plural*. Most *plural forms* use either **-s** or **-es** at the end of the word. Examples are:

    building / building**s**   cat / cat**s**   fox / fox**es**   box / box**es**

The letter **-y** in a *singular noun form* is changed to **i + es** in most cases. Examples are:

    lady / lad**ies**   baby / bab**ies**   try / tr**ies**   sky / sk**ies**

The letter **-f** or **-fe** can change to **v + es**. Examples are:

    calf / cal**ves**   knife / kni**ves**

However, there is less consistency with the letter **-f**, such as:

    hoof   hoofs   hooves   (all acceptable)

Some *nouns* have *irregular plural forms*. Examples are:

    child / **children**   goose / **geese**   tooth / **teeth**   foot / **feet**

Some *nouns* that name a *thing*, in both the *singular* and *plural form*, are spelt the same. Examples are:

    sheep / sheep   deer / deer   fun / fun   means / means

An exception: The word *'fish'* can be said as *'fishes'* in some cases:

    Many **fishes** of the sea are endangered.

✤ Countable Nouns ✤

Most *common nouns* can be categorized as *countable nouns*, also referred to as *'count nouns'*. These *nouns* are written in either the *singular* or *plural form:*

    one **cup** / twenty **cups**   one **child** / twenty **children**

The words *'some'* and *'any'* can be used with *countable nouns:*

    He's got **some** apples.   Have you got **any** books?

✤ Uncountable Nouns ✤

An *uncountable noun*, also referred to as a *'mass noun'*, cannot be *counted* and does not have a *plural form*. These types of *nouns* name a *substance* or a *concept*. Here are some examples:

air	water	**gas***(substance)	power
electricity	sugar	salt	rice

*Note: Some *nouns* that appear to be *uncountable nouns* can also be used as *countable nouns* depending on the specific word's meaning, such as:

    Going to the movies with my friends was *a* **gas**!

An *uncountable noun* may imply more than one item, but can be *voiced* collectively:

information	furniture	luggage	news
money	currency	scenery	

The *indefinite articles* *'a'* and *'an'* are not usually used with *uncountable nouns:*

    ~~*a*~~ music   ~~*an*~~ information

    but, you can write:

        A bottle of **water** or **juice**   **A** grain of **salt** or **rice**
        A piece of **news** or **information**

The words *'some'* and *'any'* are used with *uncountable nouns:*

    He's got **some** money.   Have you got **any** salt?

The words *a 'little'* and *'much'* are used with *uncountable nouns:*

    She's got *a* **little** sense.   He hasn't got **much** motivation.

✻ Collective Nouns ✻

A *collective noun* is a *'unique' noun* that reflects a *group of people, animals, objects, concepts* or *ideas*, as a single entity, such as:

People:

army	*band*	*choir*	*jury*
corporation	*crowd*	*(a) bunch*	*committee*

Animals:

flock	*colony*	*herd*	*harem*
clutch	*pride*	*tribe*	*troop*
litter	*hive*	*gaggle*	*pack*

Objects: *deck* (of cards), *crate* (of beer), ...
Abstract Ideas: *universe, ghost, spirit, love,* ...
Immeasurable Concepts: *education,* ...

✻ Concrete Nouns ✻

A *concrete noun* names a *physical object* that can usually be experienced through the senses: *hearing, sight, smell, taste* or *touch*.

A *concrete noun* can be *proper, common, countable, uncountable,* or a *collective noun* and appear in either *singular* or *plural forms*:

the Moon	student	bread	coin
perfume	police	road	staff

✻ Abstract Nouns ✻

An *abstract noun* names a *nonphysical object* that cannot be experienced through the senses: *hearing, sight, smell, taste* or *touch*. A *concrete noun* refers to a *concept, idea, emotion, belief,* or a *state of being*:

determination	contentment	enthusiasm	education
childhood	sacrifice	courage	success
graciousness	amazement	confidence	tolerance
delight	awe	trust	wisdom
humility	strength	beauty	fear

❁ Possessive Nouns ❁

A *possessive noun* is used to modify a *noun*, to indicate *ownership*. This is achieved by adding an apostrophe (') to express the possession. A *possessive noun* acts as an *adjective* to show who or what the *noun* belongs to. Examples are:

Singular nouns use an apostrophe followed by *-s*:

    John*'s* bike   Chris*'s* book
    Mount Fuji*'s* trees   My boss*'s* car

Plural nouns that do not end with an *-s* use an apostrophe followed by *-s* (~'s):

    The People*'s* Republic of Korea
    (The Republic belongs to the people.)

Plural nouns ending with *-s* use an apostrophe after *-s*:

    The student*s'* exam results
    (The exam results belong to the students.)

When two or more *nouns* possess the same thing, use an apostrophe followed by *-s*:

    Tom and Jerry*'s* adventures
    (The adventures belong to both Tom and Jerry.)

When two or more *nouns* separately possess something, then add an apostrophe to each of the *nouns* followed by *-s*:

    the boss*'s* and secretary*'s* cars
    (The boss and the secretary both have a car.)

QUOTE:
"A teacher affects eternity: he can never tell where his influence stops."

                                                                        Henry Adams

DETERMINERS (det.)

A *determiner*, also known as a *non-descriptive adjective* or *noun modifier*, is a small word that precedes a *noun*. The primary purpose of a *determiner* is to *mark a noun*, or to *'determine'* which *object, person,* or other *entity* the *noun* represents.

A *determiner* can describe how many of a particular *noun* there are or to what *degree*, with the use of *numbers* or *ordinals* (e.g. one book).

A *determiner* can also inform the reader if the *noun* is *definite* (specific or absent of doubt) or *indefinite* (general or unknown). Use a *definite determiner* when people know exactly which *noun* or *nouns* are being referred to (see Table 1.).

    Definite Article:

        the

    Possessives:

        my, your, his, her, its, our, their

    Possessive Nouns *(-'s):*

        John's..., the bus's wheel..., the children's books...

    Demonstratives:

        this, that, these, those

Table 1. Examples of Definite Determiners

	With Countable Nouns		With Uncountable Nouns
	singular	plural	singular
Definite Article: *the*	**the** cup	**the** cups	**the** furniture
Possessives	**my** cup	**my** cups	**my** furniture
Demonstratives	**this** cup	**these** cups	**this** furniture
	that cup	**those** cups	**that** furniture
Cardinal Numbers	**one** cup	**two** or **three** cups	—

An *indefinite determiner* can be used when referring to a *noun* or *nouns* in a vague manner (see Table 2.).

Indefinite Articles:
> *a, an*

Quantifiers:
> *all, some, any, every, several, many, more, most, ...*

Table 2. Examples of Indefinite Determiners

	With Countable Nouns		With Uncountable Nouns
	singular	plural	singular
Indefinite Articles: *a, an*	*a* cup *an* apple	~ cups* ~ children*	~ furniture*
Quantifiers without Comparison	—	*all* cups	*all* furniture
		some cups	*some* furniture
	any cup	*any* cups	*any* furniture
	no cup	*no* cups	*no* furniture
	another cup *each* cup *either* cup *every* cup *neither* cup *one* cup	—	—
	—	*both* cups *enough* cups *several* cups	*enough* furniture
Quantifiers with Comparison	—	*many* cups	*much* furniture
		more cups	*more* furniture
		most cups	*most* furniture
		(a) few cups	*(a) little* furniture
		fewer cups	*less* furniture
		fewest cups	*least* furniture

Note: See *Zero Articles* (*Zero Determiners*).

Determiners are organized into several classes. These classes are:

Articles

Articles are the most common *determiner class.* There are three *articles.* They are the words: *a, an, the.*

Indefinite Articles: 'a' and 'an'

The *articles 'a'* and *'an'* are called *indefinite articles* and are used to tag *nonspecific nouns.*

The *articles 'a'* and *'an'* precede a *singular noun* and are used to introduce something or someone not mentioned before. Examples are:

> I have ***a*** *very good friend* that lives nearby. He lives in ***a*** *house* two blocks from mine.
>
> I am ***an*** *English language facilitator.* I have prepared ***an*** *exam* for this week's lesson.

Table 3. Indefinite Articles: 'a' and 'an'

Use the article *'a'* preceding words that begin with a spoken consonant sound: b, c, d, f, g, h, j, k, l, m, n, p, q, r, s, t, v, w, [x*], y, z			Use the article *'an'* preceding words that begin with a spoken vowel sound: a, e, i, o, u	
** See Table 53. The Phonetic Alphabet for consonant, vowel sounds.**				
(b) **a** *boy*	(c) [k] **a** *cat*	(d) **a** *dog*	(a) [æ] **an** *apple*	(e) **an** *elf*
(f) **a** *fire*	(g) **a** *girl*	(h) **a** *hotel*	(I) **an** *Indian*	(x) [e] **an** *x-ray*
(j) [dʒ] **a** *jacket*	(k) **a** *kite*	(l) **a** *leg*	(u) [ʌ] **an** *umbrella*	(o) [əʊ] **an** *open* door
(m) **a** *mall*	(n) **a** *novel*	(p) **a** *pen*	(q) [k] **a** *quarter*	(r) **a** *room*
(s) **a** *storm*	(t) **a** *tragedy*	(v) **a** *violin*	(w) **a** *war*	(*x) See above (e)
(y) [j] **a** *yacht*	(z) **a** *zipper*			

There is an exception to the usage of the *article 'an'*. If the word following the *article 'an'* has a beginning letter that is pronounced with a sound opposite its most widely used form; a consonant beginning word pronounced like a vowel and a vowel beginning word pronounced like a consonant, then the pronunciation sound determines which *article* is used. Examples are:

A unit, not ~~*an*~~ unit. Pronounce the word unit with a beginning-letter *'y'* sound such as you-nit, so the article *'a'* is used.

A university, not ~~*an*~~ university. Pronounce the word university with a beginning-letter *'y'* sound, such as *you-ni-versity*, so the article *'a'* is used.

An hour, not ~~*a*~~ hour. Pronounce the word *hour* with a beginning-letter *'o'* as in *'our'* because of the silent *'h'*, so the article *'an'* is used.

A preceding *article* should be used according to the pronunciation sound of the specific letter being mentioned. For example, When speaking or writing about the specific letter *'e'*, the grammar written should be as follows:

When specifically speaking or writing about the letter *'e'*, then the article *'an'* is used, not the article *'a'*, such as:

An *'e'* is a vowel in the English language.

Use the article '*an*' with these letters:

an *'f'* is... an *'h'* is... an *'r'* is... an *'s'* is... an *'x'* is...

Use the article *'a'* with this letter:

a *'u'* is....

Definite Article: the

The *definite article 'the'* is used to tag something specific; an *object* or one of a number of *the same objects* that are specifically known to the person being communicated with.

The *definite article 'the'* precedes both *singular* and *plural nouns* and is used to introduce something or someone mentioned before. Examples are:

Martin Luther King Jr. (1929 – 1968) presented a historical speech. *The speech* rallied millions to take action against prejudice.

New Zealand is said to be *a* land of unbelievable beauty. *The picturesque landscapes* will take your breath away.

Table 4. Definite Article: the

Use the article 'the' (pronounced *thuh* [ðə]) preceding words that begin with a spoken consonant sound: b, c, d, f, g, h, j, k, l, m, n, p, q, r, s, t, v, w, x, y, z	Use the article 'the' (pronounced *thee* [ði *or* ði:]) preceding words that begin with a spoken vowel sound: a, e, i, o, u
The cat and **the** dog played all day.	**The** English love to drink tea and eat scones.
The boy and **the** girl are friends.	**The** car was a classic!
The [ðə] family invited **the** [ði or ði:] English girl into their home for a year. **The** [ði or ði:] Uncle of **the** [ðə] girl won her a stuffed animal at **the** [ðə] fair.	

There is an exception to the example above. Some words' beginning-letter is pronounced with a sound opposite to its most widely used form; a consonant beginning word is pronounced like a vowel and a vowel beginning word pronounced like a consonant. In these cases the pronunciation sound determines which phonetically pronounced 'the' is used, for example:

> *the [ðə]* unit, not *the [ði or ði:]* unit. The article *the [ði or ði:]* normally precedes a noun that starts with a spoken vowel sound.
>
> *the [ði:]* xray, not *the [ðə]* xray. The article *the [ðə]* normally precedes a noun that starts with a spoken consonant sound.

The above exception is also used when speaking or writing about specific letters (see Indefinite Articles 'a' and 'an').

General Article Rules: 'a', 'an', and 'the'

At the first mention of something (*subject or object*) the *article 'a'* or *'an'* is used. The second and subsequent mentions of the same 'something', then use the *article 'the'*. Examples are:

> I own **a** *car* that is very unique. **The** *car* has won many prizes.
>
> I love to eat **an** *apple* a day. **The** *apple* needs to be fresh.

✿ Zero Articles (Zero Determiners) ✿

Generally speaking, the *zero article* is where a *noun* or a *noun phrase* [where the reference is indefinite] is not preceded by the *articles a*, *an*, or *the*.

Here are some general rules for the use of *zero articles* (no article usage) preceding some *nouns*:

1. General Abstract Nouns:

    Love is all you need!

    Compassion will heal the world.

2. Names of Companies, People (in singular form) or their Titles:

    Team New Zealand won the most prestigious yachting race, the America's Cup, at least twice.

    Microsoft has led the world with new advancements in software.

3. Names of Places* (Continents, Countries, States, Provinces, Islands, Mountains, Lakes, Rivers, Towns, Cities, Roads, Streets, Avenues, Parks, Squares, Bridges, etc.):

    Australia and **New Zealand** are commonly referred to as The Land-down-under.

    Park Avenue is where I live.

    * An exception is the grouping of a particular thing:

    > **The** United States of America. (a collection of states)

    > **The** Great Lakes. **The** Cascade or **The** Rocky Mountains. (a collection of lakes or mountains)

4. Names of Meals (Breakfast, Lunch, Dinner), unless formal:

    John has **breakfast** daily, after a long 5K run.

    Dinner is ready!

    > An exception: I attended **a** banquet... (formal)

5. Names of Sports or Games:

    Rugby and **poker** are my favorite sport and game, as a spectator.

    Chess is a game I can't watch for very long.

6. A Noun followed by a Categorizing Letter or Number:

    I secured Rugby World Cup Tickets for **Section E: Row 31**.

    Auckland to Tokyo, **Flight 99**, leaves from **Gate 46**.

    I have read **page 29** of the article as you suggested.

7. Names of Diseases:

    Parkinson's is a degenerative disorder of the central nervous system that impairs motor-skills, cognitive processes, and other functions.

> ***Allergic rhinitis,*** also known as ***pollinosis***, or more commonly referred to as ***hay-fever***, is an allergic inflammation of the nasal airways, which occurs when an allergen (pollen or dust) is inhaled by a person with a sensitized immune system, which triggers antibody production.

Note: Further study is required to understand the many ways in which an *article* is or is not used with *nouns*. The above is provided as an introduction only.

❈ Demonstratives ❈

The *determiners this, that, these,* and *those* can be used as either a *demonstrative pronoun* (see *Demonstrative Pronouns*), or a *demonstrative determiner* (when it precedes a *noun*).

Table 5. Demonstratives: Pronoun vs. Determiner

this	singular	close	pronoun	I believe **this** is where I live.
			determiner	I am sure **this** car is mine.
that		far	pronoun	**That** is the book I have read.
			determiner	**That** watch is the one I want.
these	plural	close	pronoun	**These** are going to fit me.
			determiner	**These** pants shrunk.
those		far	pronoun	**Those** are fashionable outfits.
			determiner	**Those** jeans are great looking.

❈ Possessives ❈

A *possessive determiner* is sometimes called a *possessive adjective*, or simply a *possessive*. A *possessive determiner* is used in front of a *noun* to express *possession* or *belonging*. The *possessive determiners* that are used in the English language are:

    my   your   his   her   its   our   their

Here are examples of *possessives* used in a sentence:

    This is **my** car.   Is this **your** coat?
    It was **his** first time to bungee.   **Her** exam is tomorrow.

Quantifiers

A *quantifier* is a word that precedes and modifies a *noun,* to state an unknown general quantity of something, to answer the questions: *How many...,* and *How much...,* of something there is. The *quantifier* must agree with the *noun.*

Table 6. Examples of Quantifiers Used with Nouns

Quantifiers		Examples
Quantifiers used with Countable Nouns	many (of)	I do not have ***many*** *choices.*
	few (negative)	***Few*** *people* are coming. (almost nobody)
	a few (positive)	I have ***a few*** *cars.* (not many, but enough)
	a number (of)	I own ***a number of*** *houses.*
	several	I own ***several*** *championship dogs.*
	these / those	I own ***these / those*** *horses.*
	large number of	***A large number of*** *people* came.
	great number of	***A great number of*** *people* survived.
	a couple of	I own ***a couple of*** *leather jackets.*
	both	We can see ***both*** *trees* from our window.
Quantifiers used with Uncountable Nouns	much (of)	I do not have ***much*** *time* left on my exam.
	little (negative)	They had ***little*** *hope.* (almost no hope)
	a little (positive)	I have ***a little*** *money.* (enough to get by)
	a bit (of)	***A bit of*** *honey* in my tea tastes great!
	a great deal of	He is in **a *great deal of*** *trouble.*
Quantifiers used with both Countable or Uncountable Nouns	any (negative)	They do not want ***any*** *trouble.*
	any (?)	Do you want ***any*** *help* with your study?
	hardly any	***Hardly any*** *visitors* came to the show.
	some (positive)	I have ***some*** *free time* today.
	some (?)	Yes, may I have ***some*** *help* please?
	no	I have ***no*** *hope* in world peace.
	enough	There is ***enough*** *fuel* to last a week.
	enough (?)	Have you had ***enough*** *dinner?*
	none (of)	***None of*** *the children* were healthy.
	a lot of	***A lot of*** *people* like to eat strawberries.
	plenty (of)	There are ***plenty of*** *people* who can.
	lots of	There are ***lots of*** *dogs* with spots.
	most (of)	***Most of*** *the world* lacks clean water.

❋ Numbers and Ordinals ❋

A *number* and an *ordinal* is a *determiner* when it precedes a *noun*. In this position a *number* and an *ordinal* expresses the *quantity* or *sequence of* a *noun*:

Numbers Expressing Quantity:

one book, **two** books, **three** books, ...

Ordinals Expressing Sequence:

first base, **second** base, **third** base, ...

General Ordinals are not directly related to Numbers but function as Determiners:

next week, **last** month, **pervious** appointment, ...

There Is a Correct Way to Write Numbers

The number zero through nine (0 – 9) should be spelled-out, and figures are used for subsequent numbers. Here are some examples:

Five days from now I'll leave for Tokyo. Count them – **1, 2, 3, 4, 5**.

I tutor **two** boys and **three** girls each Monday after school.

There are **25** days until the New Year.

Note: There is debate over the correct writing of *numbers*. The most important strategy when deciding on how to use *numbers*, when writing, is to be consistent.

❋ Pre-determiners ❋

A *pre-determiner* precedes another *determiner*. This class of words includes:

Multipliers: *double, twice, two-times, ...*

Fractional Expressions: *one-third, three-quarters, one-half, ...*

Intensifiers: *quite, rather, such, ...*

QUOTE:

"Seldom was any knowledge given to keep, but to impart; the grace of this rich jewel is lost in concealment."

Bishop Hall

PART TWO — Adjectives (adj.)

An *adjective* is a word that describes, clarifies, or modifies a *noun* or *pronoun* by giving some information about the *noun*. Adjectives describe the *quality*, *state* or *action* that a *noun* or *pronoun* refers to. Examples are:

    Size: It is a **big** house.
    Shape: It's a **round** table.
    Age: He's an **old** man.
    Color: It's a **red** pencil.
    Origin or Religion: It's a **Buddhist** temple.
    Material: I like a **wooden** boat more than a fiberglass boat.
    Taste: I like to eat **bitter** chocolate.
    Odor: I love the smell of the **salty** sea air.
    Texture: I like to play in **squishy** mud.
    Sound: The classroom was filled with **faint** whispers.
    Number: **Few** people reach their full potential.
    Weather: It was a **clear**, **dry**, **sunny** day.

An *adjective* is also used to clarify *an opinion* or *observation* about the *noun* and its *purpose*. Examples are:

    Observation or Condition: It's a **broken** chair.
    Opinion: It's a **spiritual** journey.
    Purpose: He's a **rugby** player. (a *noun* that acts as an *adjective*)

Some *adjectives* end with *suffixes*. Examples are:

-ble:	adorable	invisible	responsible	terrible
-al:	educational	gradual	legal	essential
-an:	American	Mexican	urban	Christian
-ar:	popular	spectacular	polar	regular
-ent:	intelligent	silent	violent	excellent
-ful:	harmful	powerful	thoughtful	beautiful
-ine:	canine	feminine	masculine	divine
-ile:	agile	docile	fertile	hostile
-ive:	informative	native	talkative	active
-ous:	cautious	dangerous	enormous	famous
-ic or *-ical:*	athletic	energetic	scientific	magical
-ly or *-y:*	lovely	lonely	guilty	hungry
-some:	awesome	handsome	lonesome	wholesome
-less:	priceless	careless	homeless	blameless

Note: Many *adjectives* also end with **-ate, -ary,** and **-y,** but many *nouns* and *adverbs* also end with **-y,** also many *nouns* end with **-ary,** and many *nouns* and *verbs* also end with **-ate**, so it can be confusing.

Other possible adjective endings may be:

-like:	childlike	fishlike	wifelike	zombielike
-ish:	foolish	biggish	blackish	dullish
-en:	golden	debt-ridden	broken	unproven

�֍ Adjectives Before Nouns or After Verbs �֍

An *adjective* can come before a *noun*. If a word ends in any *suffix*, such as: **-ate, -ary,** or **-y,** the word can be identified as an *adjective* by where the word is and what the word is doing in the sentence. If a word is placed immediately before a *noun*, especially if the word comes between an *article* (a, an, the), a *demonstrative* (this, that, these, those), a *possessive determiner* (my, your, his, her, its, our, their), or a *quantifier* (few, many, most, several, each, every, some, all, any, etc.) and a *noun*, then it's probably an *adjective*. Here are some examples:

Article: **The <u>dirty</u> boy** needed a bath.

> The word <u>dirty</u> comes between the article **The** and the noun **boy**, so the word <u>dirty</u> is an adjective.

Demonstrative: Did you see **that <u>savvy</u> model?**

> The word <u>savvy</u> comes between the demonstrative **that** and the noun **model**, so the word <u>savvy</u> is an adjective.

Possessive: These are **my <u>old</u> clothes.**

> The word <u>old</u> comes between the possessive determiner **my** and the noun **clothes**, so the word <u>old</u> is an adjective.

Quantifier: We have **few <u>ordinary</u> weekends.**

> The word <u>ordinary</u> comes between the quantifier **few** and the noun **weekends**, so the word <u>ordinary</u> is an adjective.

An *adjective* [or a *noun* or any word that acts as a *noun* or *adjective*] that serves as a *complement to a verb* and qualifies *the direct object* is called an *objective complement*. An *objective complement* provides additional information about the *object* and is placed after the *verb* and *object*. Examples are:

subject	+	*verb (verb phrase)*	+	*object*	+	*adjective*
My Mom		keeps		her kitchen		spotless
I		like		my tea		black

Not all *complements* are *adjectives*. In the example directly below, the words *intelligent, handsome, confident,* and *thin,* are *adjectives* that complement the verb, but the phrases <u>friends for five years</u> and <u>my best friend</u> are both *noun phrases* that also complement the verb.

    He is **intelligent**, **handsome** and **confident**.   She is **thin**.

    We've been <u>friends for five years</u>.   You were <u>my best friend</u>.

Here are some tips for identifying *complementing adjectives* and *noun phrases:*

1. If the *complement* is only one word, it's most likely an *adjective*.
2. If the *complements* are a list of words, those words are most likely *adjectives*.
3. If an *article* (a, an, the) or a *possessive* (my, mine, your, yours, his, her, hers, its, our, ours, their, theirs) is present, then it most likely is a *noun phrase*.

✤ Comparative and Superlative Adjectives ✤

One-syllable Adjectives

A *one-syllable comparative* and *superlative adjective* is formed by adding *-er* for the *comparative form* and *-est* for the *superlative form*. However, some exceptions are as follows:

    If a *one-syllable adjective* ends with *-e*

        Comparative Form: add *-r*

        Superlative Form: add *-st*

    If a *one-syllable adjective* ends with a single consonant with a vowel before it:

        Comparative Form: double the consonant and add *-er*

        Superlative Form: double the consonant and add *-est*

Table 7. One-syllable Comparative and Superlative Adjectives

One-syllable Adjectives	Comparative Form	Superlative Form
tall	taller	tallest
short	shorter	shortest
thin	thinner	thinnest

One-syllable Adjectives Ending with *-e*	Comparative Form	Superlative Form
large	larger	largest
wise	wiser	wisest
Ending with a single consonant with a vowel before It		
big	bigger	biggest
fat	fatter	fattest

Two-syllable Adjectives

A *two-syllable comparative* and *superlative adjective* is modified by adding the word '*more*' for the *comparative form* and '*most*' for the *superlative form*. However, some exceptions are as follows:

    If an *adjective* ends with *-y*

        Comparative Form: change *-y* to *i + er*
        Superlative Form: change *-y* to *i + est*

    If a *two-syllable adjective* ends with *-le*

        Comparative Form: add *-r*
        Superlative Form: add *-st*

    If a *two-syllable adjective* ends with *-ow*

        Comparative Form: add *-er*
        Superlative Form: add *-est*

Table 8. Two-syllable Comparative and Superlative Adjectives

Two-syllable Adjectives	Comparative Form	Superlative Form
famous	more famous	most famous
peaceful	more peaceful	most peaceful
Ending with *-y*		
happy	happier	happiest
lonely	lonelier	loneliest
Ending with *-le* or *-ow*		
gentle	gentler	gentlest
narrow	narrower	narrowest

Two-syllable Adjectives	Comparative Form	Superlative Form
likely	likelier more likely	likeliest most likely
polite	politer more polite	politest most polite
simple	simpler more simple	simplest most simple

Adjectives of Three or More Syllables

A *comparative* and *superlative adjective* of *three* or *more syllables*, is modified by adding the word *'more'* for the *comparative form* and *'most'* for the *superlative form*.

Table 9. Comparative and Superlative Adjectives of Three or More Syllables

Adjectives of Three or More Syllables	Comparative Form	Superlative Form
fortunate	more fortunate	most fortunate
intelligent	more intelligent	most intelligent

Irregular Adjectives

There are some *adjectives* that are *irregular*. These *adjectives* do not follow the standard rules.

Table 10. Irregular Adjectives

Irregular Adjectives	Comparative Form	Superlative Form
bad / ill / badly	worse	worst
good / well	better	best
little	less	least
many (countable)	more	most
much (uncountable)	more	most

Meaning Differences with Adjectives

Table 11. Examples of Meaning Differences with Adjectives

	Comparative	Superlative	Description
far	farther (than) farther (up)	farthest	physical distance
	further / to consider further	furthest / furthest from the ...	limited to the figurative, abstract senses, extent
late	later	latest	related to time or age
	latter	last	related to order
old	older	oldest	people or things of age
	elder	eldest	senior or older person

Correct Adjective Order

When several *adjectives* in a sentence are listed, there's a specific order they must be written or spoken in. Michael Swan (Practical English Usage, Oxford University Press, 1997) writes, "Unfortunately, the rules for adjective order are very complicated, and different grammars disagree about the details" (p. 8).

Although this may be true, here is the most commonly used basic order, with examples:

determiner + judgment / attitude / opinion / feeling + size / length / height + shape + age + color + origin + religion + material + purpose + noun

1. Determiner:
   - Article: *a, an, the*
   - Possessive Determiner: my, your, *his, her, its, our, their*
   - Number or Ordinal: *two, twenty, first, second, 1st, 2nd, 3rd, ...*
   - Demonstrative: *this, that, these, those, ...*
2. Judgment, Attitude, Opinion, or Feeling: *beautiful, expensive, silly, weird, boring, magnificent, serene, breathtaking, ...*
3. Size, Length, and Height: *long, huge, tiny, tall, short, ...*
4. Shape and Width: *round, circular, oblong, narrow, ...*
5. Age: *young, old, antique, ...*

6. Color: *green, purple, ...*
7. Origin or Nationality: *British, Australian, American, ...*
8. Religion: *Buddhist, Muslim, Christian, Hindu, ...*
9. Material: *cotton, gold, diamond, wooden, ...*
10. Purpose or Type (*qualifier*): *sleeping, ...* [*sleeping* bag]

Notes:

1. If *adjectives* are listed after the *'be'* verb as *complements*, and a *qualifier* is used, the *qualifier* will precede the *noun*. Commas should be used to separate *adjectives* within the *complement* with the two final *adjectives* being separated by the conjunction *'and'*.

    My *sleeping* bag *is* warm, big, old, blue and waterproof.

2. **Caution.** The overuse of *adjectives* [also true for the overuse of *adverbs*] may overwhelm the recipient and weaken the overall effect of the communication.

QUOTE:

"To write or even speak English is not a science but an art. There are no reliable words. Whoever writes English is involved in a struggle that never lets up even for a sentence. He is struggling against vagueness, against obscurity, against the lure of the decorative adjective, against the encroachment of Latin and Greek, and, above all, against the worn-out phrases and dead metaphors with which the language is cluttered up."

George Orwell, English Novelist and Essayist (1903-1959)

PART THREE — Pronouns (pron.)

A *pronoun* is a word that substitutes a *noun* or *noun phrase*. A *pronoun* can be used as the sentence's *subject, object,* or *complement* and can also follow a *preposition*.

 Personal Pronouns

A *personal pronoun* is used as a substitute word in place of a *person* or *people* who are being talked about.

Table 12. Personal Pronouns

Subjective: acts as the subject of the sentence	singular	I, you, he, she, it and one
		I went to the mountain. *One* has to be diligent with one's money.
	plural	you, we and they
		They go to church every Sunday.
Objective: acts as the object of the verb or the preposition	singular	me, you, him, her, it and one
		Can you help *me* to find the bank?
	prep.	This is confidential between *you* and *me*.
	plural	you, us and them
		Could you ask *them* to join *us* for lunch?
	prep.	Please take a picture of *us* with *them*.
Possessive: refers to something owned by someone or something previously mentioned	mostly singular	mine, yours, his and hers
		Whose key is this, *mine* or *yours*?
	mostly plural	yours, ours and theirs
		Our children go to school by bus, but theirs go by car.
Reflexive: refers back to the subject of the clause in which they are used	singular	himself, herself, itself, myself, oneself and yourself
		Henry taught *himself* to drive.
	plural	ourselves, themselves and yourselves
		We helped *ourselves* to dinner.

First, Second or Third-Person

First Person

When talking about yourself to another person, refer to yourself as *I, me, my, mine,* or *myself*. Examples are:

    I went to the park.   ***not***   (your name) went to the park.

    David likes ***me***, not her!   John gave ***mine*** to her.

Second Person

When talking directly to another person (physically present or by phone), with that person as the subject, you would start the conversation by mentioning that person by their name (on the first occasion [as a point of reference]) and then subsequently refer to them as *you, your, yours*, or *yourself*. Examples are:

    Jim, are ***you*** ready to go? ***not*** Is (their name) ready to go?

    Mary, are ***you*** hungry? ***You*** said ***you*** were, so let's go eat!

Third Person

When talking about another person who is not present, you would start the conversation by mentioning that person by their name (on the first occasion [as a point of reference]), and then subsequently refer to them as *he, him, his, himself*, or *she, her, hers, herself*. Examples are:

    Bob went to the zoo. ***He*** fed the deer and then ~~*he*~~ went home.

Table 13. First, Second, or Third Person Pronoun Usage

		$1^{st}, 2^{nd}, 3^{rd}$ Person	Subject	Object	Possessive		Reflective
					det.	Pron.	
Singular		1st	I	me	my	mine	myself
		2nd	you	you	your	yours	yourself
	3rd	male	he	him	his	his	himself
		female	she	her	her	hers	herself
		neuter	it	it	its	its	itself
		generic	one	one	one's	—	oneself
Plural		1st	we	us	our	ours	ourselves
		2nd	you	you	your	yours	yourselves
		3rd	they	them	their	theirs	themselves

Demonstrative Pronouns

A *demonstrative pronoun* substitutes and points attention toward a specific *person, animal, place,* or *thing* that is clearly understood or has been mentioned previously. There are four common *demonstrative pronouns:*

　　　this　　　　　　*that*　　　　　　*these*　　　　　　*those*

Table 14. Demonstrative Pronouns

		this or *that*
Singular	subject	**This** has been a fantastic year for Warren Buffett and his team. **That** is the room you should decorate for the job fair.
	object	Would you buy **this**? The new product made **that** obsolete.
	object of the preposition	Does the tie you bought go with **this**? Kim will upgrade the new administrative software on **that** soon.
		these or *those*
Plural	subject	**These** are the computer geeks that have revolutionized social-media. **Those** that wanted the next model must wait another week.
	object	Will Brad complete **these** before noon? Jacob gave **those** to the carpenter.
	object of the preposition	Please read over **these** before the deadline. Maryanne can work with **those**.

QUOTE:

"Do not be surprised when those who ignore the rules of grammar also ignore the law. After all, the law is just so much grammar."

　　　　　　　　　　　　　　　　　　　　　　　　Robert Brault

A *demonstrative pronoun* may act as an *adjective* (*demonstrative determiner*) when it is used to clarify a *noun*, rather than to substitute it. For example:

Table 15. Demonstrative Pronouns Acting Like an Adjective

	Demonstrative	Examples
this	pronoun	***This*** will save us from disaster.
	determiner	***This*** road is a dead end.
that	pronoun	***That*** is not what I asked you.
	determiner	***That*** solution will work well.
these	pronoun	***Those*** will confuse us all.
	determiner	***Those*** suggestions are the best I've heard all week.
those	pronoun	***These*** tasted so sweet.
	determiner	***These*** candies are delicious.

> ***QUOTE:***
>
> *"I is the first letter of the alphabet, the first word of the language, the first thought of the mind, the first object of affection. In grammar it is a pronoun of the first person and singular number. Its plural is said to be 'we' but how can there be more than one myself is doubtless clearer to the grammarians than it is to the author of this incomparable dictionary. Conception of two myselfs is difficult, but fine. The frank yet graceful use of 'I' distinguishes a good writer from the bad; the latter carries it with the manner of a thief trying to cloak his loot."*
>
> Ambrose Bierce, Writer, Journalist and Editor (1842-1914)

✿ Relative Pronouns ✿

In most cases a *relative pronoun* begins a *subordinate clause* and connects that clause to another *noun* that precedes it in the same sentence. There are several main *relative pronouns* in modern English.

Table 16. Relative Pronouns

who*	\multicolumn{2}{c}{Generally used only for people:}	
	subjective	The person **who** phoned me last weekend is my dad.
	objective	The man **who** I talked to at the hardware store is my uncle.
whom*	objective	The person **whom** I nominated as chairman is very trustworthy.
that	\multicolumn{2}{c}{Can be used for people and things:}	
	subjective	The noisy dog **that** barked all night belongs to my neighbor.
	objective	The team **that** I cheered for this season is my favorite.
which*	\multicolumn{2}{c}{Refers to things, qualities and ideas and never for people:}	
	subjective	This is my uncle's antique car **which** doesn't work properly.
	objective	This is my mom's mobile phone **which** I borrowed last night.
whose*	\multicolumn{2}{c}{Refers to people, things, qualities, and ideas:}	
	possessive	I have beautiful triplets **whose** names are Peter, Paul and Mary.
whoever	\multicolumn{2}{c}{whoever, whomever, whatever, whichever}	
	\multicolumn{2}{c}{Peter will throw the ball to **whomever** is ready to catch it.}	

*These words can also be used as *interrogative pronouns;* see *interrogative pronouns* in the next section.

❊ Interrogative Pronouns ❊

An *interrogative pronoun* is similar to a *relative pronoun*; the difference is that it asks a question (?) and is normally the first word in that sentence. An *interrogative pronoun* represents the unknown.

Table 17. Interrogative Pronouns

who* people	subject	Q: **Who** is the greatest boxer of all time?
		A: Either *Muhammad Ali* or *Sugar Ray Lenard* is the greatest boxer of all time.
	object	Q: **Who** do you mentor?
		A: I mentor *special-needs children*.
	complement	Q: **Who** are his teachers?
		A: They are *John and Jack*.
	with a preposition	Q: **Who** were you fishing *with*?
		A: (*With*) *a coworker of my Dad's*.
whom people	object (formal)	Q: **Whom** do you know?
		A: I know *Mr. Rogers*.
	after a preposition	Q: *To* **whom** was the exam submitted?
		A: (*To*) *Professor John Woods*.
what* non-human	subject	Q: **What's** happened here?
		A: *The pipes burst*.
	object	Q: **What** did you achieve last year?
		A: I achieved *four Olympic gold medals*.
which* people or non-human	subject	Q: **Which** is yours?
		A: *This book* is mine.
	object	Q: **Which** will the teacher mark first?
		A: The teacher will mark and return *the second-grade exams* first.
whose people possessive form	subject	Q: There are several exams yet to be turned in. **Whose** is missing?
		A: *Matthew's* exam is missing.
	object	Q: We've bought new shoes. **Whose** do you like the most?
		A: I like *hers*.

29

* The *suffix –ever* is sometimes used to form a compound word with some of these pronouns: *who, what, and which.* They are used to emphasize the situation or to show reflection [deeper thought]. Examples are:

> **Whoever** would want to paint their house that terrible color?
>
> **Whatever** did they do to make the authorities react as they did?
>
> I could never decide! **Whichever** will you choose?

❋ Indefinite Pronouns ❋

An *indefinite pronoun* is vague in nature and doesn't point to any particular *noun*. Most are either *singular* or *plural;* however, some *indefinite pronouns* can be *singular* in one context and *plural* in another.

Table 18. Indefinite Pronouns

Singular	*another, anybody, anyone, anything, each, either, enough, everybody, everyone, everything, less, little, much, neither*, no-one*, nobody*, nothing*, one, other, somebody, someone, something*	
	I enjoyed that cake. May I have **another**? Can **anyone** direct me to the library?	
Plural	*both, few or fewer, many, others, several*	
	Both were equally responsible for the company's success. **Fewer** are interested in classical music in recent years.	
Singular or Plural	all, any, more, most, none*, some, such	
	singular	There is a lot of furniture in the showroom; **some** is a real bargain.
	plural	There are many chairs in the showroom; **some** are a real bargain.

* These *indefinite pronouns* are also referred to as *negative pronouns;* see *negative pronouns* in the next section.

✽ Negative Pronouns ✽

A *negative pronoun* refers to a *negative noun phrase*.

Table 19. Negative Pronouns Used in the English Language

		neither*, no one, nobody, nothing
Singular	people or non-human	Tom and James took the exam. **Neither** passed. Do you like cats or dogs? **Neither** interests me!
	people	**No one** came forward to answer the question. **Nobody** showed up.
	non-human	The lions did **nothing** all day but sleep.
Singular or Plural		*none*
	people or non-human	**None** (of the furniture) is on sale. **None** (of them) show the slightest interest in the history of Jazz music.

***Neither** is the negative form of **either** and can be used before a *noun*.

✽ Reciprocal Pronouns ✽

There are only two *reciprocal pronouns*, 'each other' and 'one another'. Both of these *reciprocal pronouns* have the same meaning. They are used when two or more subjects are interacting with or have a mutual relationship with each other.

Gerald and Shirley have been married to **each other** for 50+ years.

Gerald and Shirley have been married to **one another** for 50+ years.

QUOTE:

"Try to use the pronoun 'we' instead of 'you' and speak about the intended result instead of the failed attempt."

Terri Lonier

PART FOUR — Verbs (v.)

Most *verbs* are *action verbs*, also referred to as *dynamic verbs. Verbs* are things that a person can *'do'* or ask someone else to *'do'* (play, run, talk, see, etc.), or give the idea of *'existence'* or *'state of being'* (be, exist, seem, belong, etc.), for example:

Chris ***read*** a book last night. (action)

Krystal ***seems*** intelligent. (state)

A *verb* follows the *subject* of a sentence and can have an ***-ing, -ed,*** or ***-s*** word ending added to it, for example:

Kelvyn *(subj.) play**ed** (v.)* soccer *(n.).*

A verb changes form to inform the reader or listener as to when something occurred (verb tenses of time), such as:

write (s)	*wrote*	*written*	*writing*
play (s)	*played*	*playing*	

Main (Principal) Verbs

A *main verb,* also known as a *principal verb,* is the simplest 'stripped down' *verb form* (base or root word). A *verb* express *a continual* or *habitual action*, *general truth / fact*, or a *state of being* in a sentence. The *main verb* functions as the *present tense form* for all persons and numbers, but not the *third-person singular*, which uses the ***-s form***. Examples are:

*she **writes*** *he **plays***

Note: A *main verb* is the first *word form* listed in most English language dictionaries. The *main verb* can have *morphemes* called *affixes* attached to them either at the beginning of the *verb*, called *prefixes* (***re-***, ***in-***, ***un-***, ***co-***, ***miss-***, ***un-***), or the ending, called *suffixes* (***-ing***, ***-ion***, ***-ation***, ***-able***, ***-ment***). The addition of such *morphemes* may change the word's form. Examples are:

believe (v.), *believ**ing*** (n., adj.), ***un**believ**able*** (adj.)

Active and Passive Voice

Voice refers to whether the *subject* of a sentence is performing the action, or is having the action done to it.

Active voice, also referred to as *normal voice,* refers to the <u>*subject*</u> performing the action, such as:

<u>Sir Edmond Hillary</u> ***climbed*** Mount Everest.

The *passive voice* places the entity that receives the action in the *subject* position of the sentence. This shifts the focus from the entity performing the action to the entity receiving the action. The construction of a *passive voice* sentence and examples are:

>subject **+ auxiliary verb (be) +** main verb *(past participle*)*
>The classroom *was* cleaned* by John.
>
>>*The *main verb* is **always** in its *past participle form.*

The Conjugation for Passive Voice

The *passive voice* can be formed in any *tense* or *future time* by following these simple examples (also see Table 20.):

>Present Simple: ~ ***am / are / is +*** *past participle*
>Present Continuous: ~ ***is being / are being +*** *past participle*
>Present Perfect: ~ ***has been / have been +*** *past participle*
>Present Perfect Continuous: ~ **has / have been being +** *past participle*
>Past Simple: ~ ***was / were +*** *past participle*
>Past Continuous: ~ ***was being / were being +*** *past participle*
>Past Perfect: ~ ***had been +*** *past participle*
>Past Perfect continuous: ~ ***had been being +*** *past participle*
>Future Simple: ~ ***will be +*** *past participle*
>Future Continuous: ~ ***will be being +*** *past participle*
>Future Perfect: ~ ***will have been +*** *past participle*
>Future Perfect Continuous: ~ ***will have been being +*** *past participle*

Note: *Modal verbs* can be used in the *passive voice*, such as: ...***can be*** loved... or ...***might / could have been*** avoided...

Table 20. Conjugation (link) for Passive Voice

Tense or future time		Examples	
Present	simple	active: passive:	I call the cat Bonnie. *The cat **is** called Bonnie.*
	continuous	active: passive:	The staff are dressing mannequins. *Mannequins **are being** dressed.*
	perfect	active: passive:	We have invited our mates as well. *Our mates **have been** invited as well.*
	perfect continuous	active: passive:	Fred has been cleaning his car. *His car **has been being** cleaned.*

33

Tense or future time		Examples	
Past	simple	active:	I named the horse Trigger.
		passive:	*The horse **was** <u>named</u> Trigger.*
	continuous	active:	Someone was making the coffee.
		passive:	*The coffee **was being** <u>made</u>.*
	perfect	active:	Peter had completed filming his documentary on Maori culture.
		passive:	*Filming his documentary on Maori culture **had been** <u>completed</u>.*
	perfect continuous	active:	Craig had been fueling the jet.
		passive:	*The jet **had been being** <u>fueled</u>.*
Future	simple	active:	The woman will wink at the child.
		passive:	*The child **will be** <u>winked</u> at.*
	continuous	active:	Jane will be driving the car.
		passive:	*The car **will be being** <u>driven</u>.*
	perfect	active:	Gary will have packed his lunch.
		passive:	*His lunch **will have been** <u>packed</u>.*
	perfect continuous	active:	I will have been soaking my new dentures.
		passive:	*My new dentures **will have been being** <u>soaked</u>.*

❈ Auxiliary Verbs ❈

An *auxiliary verb*, also known as a *helping verb*, determines the *mood*, *voice*, or *tense*, modifying the meaning of the *main verb* that they accompany in a *verb phrase*.

Primary Auxiliary Verbs:

'be' forms: *am, are, is, was, were, been, being*

'do' forms: *do, does, did*

'have' forms: *have, has, had, having*

Modal Auxiliary Verbs:

can	*could*	*may*	*might*	*will*
would	*shall*	*should*	*must*	*ought (to)*

Primary Auxiliary Verbs (be, do, have)

A *primary auxiliary verb* can be used as follows:

be*:   *be* + present participle (verb + -ing) = *progressive form*
           be + past participle = *passive (voice)*

do*:   *do, does,* or *did* + the basic (base) *verb form* can be used in *negative, emphasis,* or *interrogative* sentences.

have*: *have, has,* or *had* + past participle = *perfect form*

           *can also be used as a *main verb*.

Table 21. Primary Auxiliary Verbs

Primary Auxiliary (Helping) Verb Forms				
Base Form	Present Form	Past Form	Past Participle	Present Participle
be	am, are, is	was, were	been	being
do	do, does	did	—	—
have	have, has	had	—	having

Note: *Contracted verb forms* can be stacked. Examples are:

~ woud have:

     I'd've told her to study if I had been there.

~ will have:

     He'll've arrived by the time the presentation starts.

Primary Auxiliary Verb *'be'* and Its Forms

The *primary auxiliary verb* **'be'** and its forms are used to create the *continuous / progressive form* of a *verb phrase*, indicating either a *short-term action* or an *action* that is still in progress, or to create a *passive voice*. Examples are:

     He **is** <u>watching</u> football on TV. (continuous / progressive form)

     Zebras **are** <u>eaten</u> by lions. (passive voice)

Here is the *main verb 'be'* and the different forms of the *'be'* *auxiliary verb* with examples:

The basic or base form (main verb):

    be   In use:

        To **be** or *not to* **be** kind is the question.

The present continuous forms and passive voice [**be** auxiliary *verb*]:

    am: Used with the word *'I'* as the *subject:*

        I **am** <u>playing</u> football now. (affirmative)

        I **am** <u>called</u> lucky by my friends. (passive voice)

        Am *I* <u>doing</u> this how you wanted? (interrogative)

    Use *I'm* as the contracted form of *I* **am**:

        I'm <u>eating</u> lunch now.

    Use **am not** for *negative sentences:*

        I **am not** <u>dancing</u> tonight… never … ~~amn't~~ dancing…

    are: Used with the words **we, you, they** or a *plural noun phrase* as the *subject:*

        They **are** <u>smiling</u> at me. (affirmative)

        They **are** <u>shown</u> regularly. (passive voice)

        Are you <u>coming</u> to my party this weekend? (interrogative)

        My twins **are** <u>wearing</u> the same clothes. (plural noun phrase)

    Use **~'re** as the contracted form of **we are, you are** or **they are**:

        We're <u>painting</u> the house next week.

        You're <u>going</u> to the park on Saturday.

        They're <u>cooking</u> New Zealand spring lamb.

    Use **are not**, or the contracted form **aren't**, for *negative sentences:*

        We **are not** (aron't) <u>joking</u> around.

        You **are not** (aren't) <u>flying</u> due to heavy rain.

        They **are not** (aren't) <u>laughing</u> at my joke.

is: Used with the words **he**, **she**, **it** or a *singular noun phrase* as the *subject*:

> He **is** <u>reading</u> a book. (affirmative)
> He **is** <u>loaded</u> with homework. (passive voice)
> What **is** she <u>doing</u>? (interrogative)
> My patient **is** <u>wearing</u> a hospital gown.
> (singular noun phrase)

Use **~'s** as the contracted form of **he is, she is** or **it is**:

> He**'s** <u>practicing</u> the piano.
> She**'s** <u>studying</u> English now.
> It**'s** <u>raining</u> now.

Use **is not**, or the contracted form **isn't**, for *negative sentences*:

> He **is not** (isn't) <u>being</u> very nice at all.
> She **is not** (isn't) <u>wearing</u> her hat.
> It **is not** (isn't) <u>growing</u> well.

The past continuous forms and passive voice [**be** auxiliary verb]:

was: Used with the words **I, he, she, it** or a *singular noun phrase* as the *subject*:

> I **was** <u>making</u> cookies with my grandma. (affirmative)
> I **was** <u>worked</u> to the bone. (passive voice)
> **Was** it <u>snowing</u> all night? (interrogative)
> My wife **was** <u>snoring</u> all night. (singular noun phrase)

Note: There is no contracted form for **was**.

Use **was not**, or the contracted form **wasn't**, for *negative sentences*:

> I **was not** (wasn't) <u>having</u> fun at the opera.
> He **was not** (wasn't) <u>running</u> the race in top form.
> It **was not** (wasn't) <u>smoking</u> last time I checked.

were: Used with the words **we, you, they** or a *plural noun phrase* as the *subject*:

> We **were** <u>cheering</u> for our favorite team. (affirmative)
> You **were** <u>choked</u> by the smoke. (passive)
> **Were** you <u>drinking</u> all night? (interrogative)
> My parents **were** <u>bathing</u> at the spa last week.
> (plural noun phrase)

Note: There is no contracted form for **were**.

Use **were not**, or the contracted form **weren't**, for *negative sentences*:

> We **were not** (weren't) <u>serving</u> pasta.
> You **were not** (weren't) <u>singing</u> very well.
> They **were not** (weren't) <u>looking</u> at me.

Primary Auxiliary Verb *'do'* and Its Forms

The *primary auxiliary verb* **'do'** and its forms are used to create *negatives, interrogatives*, and to show *emphasis*. Examples are:

> I **do not** <u>like</u> cabbage. (negative)
>
> **Do** you <u>work</u> for Google? (interrogative)
>
> I **did** <u>say</u> to you wait for me! (emphasis)

Here is the *main verb* **'do'** and the different forms of the **'do'** *auxiliary verb* with examples:

The basic or base form (main verb):

> **do**   In use:
>
> > When I get home from school I **do** my homework.

The present simple forms [**do** *auxiliary verb*]:

> **do:**   Used with the **words I, you, we, they** or a *plural noun phrase* as the *subject*.
>
> An affirmative sentence doesn't normally use the *auxiliary verb* **'do'** unless the word **'do'** is used for *emphasis*:
>
> > I like ice-cream. Or, I **do** <u>like</u> ice-cream. (emphasis)
> > My friends **do** <u>enjoy</u> clubbing. (plural noun phrase)
>
> Use **do** in an interrogative (question):
>
> > **Do** you <u>avoid</u> eating spicy food?
>
> **Note**: There is no contracted form for **do**.
>
> Use **do not**, or the contracted form **don't**, for *negative sentences*:
>
> > I **do not** (don't) <u>consider</u> chocolate as junk food.

does: Used with the words *he, she, it* or a *singular noun phrase* as the *subject*.

An affirmative sentence doesn't normally use the *auxiliary verb* **'does'** unless the word **'does'** is used for *emphasis:*

She sleeps often. Or, she **does** <u>sleep</u> often. (emphasis).

His dog **does** <u>dig</u> in my garden…bugger! (singular noun phrase)

Use **does** in an interrogative (question):

Does he <u>visit</u> his parents on the weekend?

Note: There is no contracted form for **does**.

Use **does not**, or the contracted form **doesn't**, for *negative sentences:*

He **does not** (doesn't) <u>swim</u> in the ocean.

The past simple form [*do auxiliary verb*]:

did: Used with the words *I, you, we, they, he, she, it* or a *noun phrase* as the *subject*.

An affirmative sentence doesn't normally use the *auxiliary verb* **'did'** unless the word **'did'** is used for *emphasis:*

He drove me crazy. Or, He **did** <u>drive</u> me crazy. (emphasis)

My students **did** <u>participate</u> well. (noun phrase)

Use **did** in an interrogative (question):

Did they <u>call</u> me?

Note: There is no contracted form for **did**.

Use **did not**, or the contracted form **didn't**, for *negative sentences:*

I **did not** (didn't) <u>shoot</u> the ball at the buzzer.

Primary Auxiliary Verb *'have'* and Its Forms

The *primary auxiliary verb* **'have'** and its forms are used to create *affirmatives, negatives,* and *interrogatives* using the *perfect form* of *main verbs.* Examples are:

I **have not** <u>cleaned</u> my room yet. (negative)

Have you <u>answered</u> the questionnaire? (interrogative)

Here is the *main verb 'have'* and the different forms of the *'have' auxiliary verb* with examples:

The basic or base form (main verb):

have In use:

To **have** or not to **have** happiness is but a choice.

The present perfect forms [**have** auxiliary verb]:

have: Used with the words *I, you, we, they* or a *plural noun phrase* as the *subject:*

I **have** <u>enjoyed</u> painting all my life. (affirmative)

Their children **have** been <u>talking</u> all night.
(plural noun phrase)

Use **have** in an interrogative (question):

Have you <u>seen</u> the new action movie?

Use **~'ve** as the contracted form of *I have, we have, you have* or *they have:*

*I***'ve** <u>filmed</u> many animal behaviors.

*You***'ve** <u>encouraged</u> me often.

*They***'ve** <u>drained</u> the pool to clean it.

Use **have not**, or the contracted form **haven't**, for *negative sentences:*

I **have not** (haven't) <u>extended</u> an invitation to him yet.

We **have not** (haven't) <u>gathered</u> here to be passive.

You **have not** (haven't) <u>healed</u> well.

has: Used with the words *he, she, it* or a *singular noun phrase* as the *subject:*

He **has** <u>instructed</u> me well. (affirmative)

My flight **has** <u>been</u> delayed. (singular noun phrase)

Use *has* in an interrogative (question):

Has he <u>traveled</u> extensively?

Use **~'s** as the contracted form of *he has, she has* or *It has:*

*He***'s** <u>played</u> on this team for months.

*She***'s** <u>won</u> the beauty-pageant three years running.

*It***'s** <u>worked</u> out well for everyone.

Use **has not**, or the contracted form **hasn't**, for *negative sentences:*

> He **has not** (hasn't) <u>listened</u> to me at all.
>
> She **has not** (hasn't) <u>changed</u> her opinion.
>
> It **has not** (hasn't) <u>nested</u> in that tree this year.

The past perfect form [**have** auxiliary verb]:

had Used with the words *I, you, we, they, he, she, it* or a *noun phrase* as the *subject:*

> They **had** <u>climbed</u> down from the tree. (affirmative)
>
> My girlfriend **had** <u>been</u> late. (noun phrase)

Use **had** in an interrogative (question):

> **Had** she <u>memorized</u> her notes?

Use **-'d** as the contracted form of **I had, you had, we had, they had, he had, she had** or **it had**:

> I**'d** <u>parked</u> there before.
>
> They**'d** <u>performed</u> to the best of their ability.
>
> He**'d** <u>queued</u> for hours in the rain.

Use **had not**, or the contracted form **hadn't**, for *negative sentences:*

> I **had not** (hadn't) <u>remembered</u> a thing.
>
> He **had not** (hadn't) <u>recognized</u> her.
>
> You **had not** (hadn't) <u>telephoned</u> beforehand!

Modal Auxiliary Verbs

A *modal auxiliary verb* is used to modify the meaning of the *main verb* allowing the expression of *necessity, obligation,* or *possibility*. A *modal auxiliary verb* can also form a *question* and a *negative*. The *modal auxiliary verbs* are:

> *can, could,* and *might*
>
> *may* and *must*
>
> *shall, should,* and *ought (to)*
>
> *will*
>
> *would*

Each of the 10 *modal auxiliary verbs* have different strengths in their meaning with other similar modals, reflecting *stronger* or *weaker effect*.

Table 22. Modal Auxiliary Verbs

\multicolumn{6}{c}{Examples of Modal Auxiliary Verbs (also see next section)}
can	cannot	can't	could	could not	couldn't
may	may not	mayn't	might	might not	mightn't
must	must not	mustn't	ought (to)	ought not	oughtn't
shall	shall not	shan't	should	should not	shouldn't
will	will not	won't	would	would not	wouldn't

Can, Could and *Might* - Used in an *affirmative* and *negative statement*, or *interrogative* (can and could mainly) with the words *I, you, we, they, he, she,* and *it,* or a *singular* or *plural noun phrase* as the *subject*.

Table 23. Modal Auxiliary Verbs 'Can', 'Could' and 'Might'

Modal	Negative	Meanings	Examples
can	cannot / can't	ability	*I **can** speak* English well.
		permission	***Can** we play* lacrosse today?
		possibility	You **can** ask for a raise if you like.
		request or offer	***Can** you help* me, please? / ***Can** I help* you?
could	could not / couldn't	past ability	He **could** play football years ago, but his age has caught up to him.
		permission	I was wondering, **could** *I borrow* your car?
		future possibility	It **could** *rain* this afternoon. I suppose *I **could** take* my umbrella.
		request	I understand you may be busy, but **could** *you go* and buy some milk?
		suggestion	Q: What can I do to improve? A: *You **could** study* more!
might	might not / mightn't	probability	*I **might** win* the lottery.
		possibility in the past	If you had studied more, *you **might** have passed* the exam!

May and *Must* - Used in an *affirmative* and *negative statement,* or *interrogative* with the words *I, you, we, they, he, she,* and *it,* or a *singular* or *plural noun phrase* as the *subject.*

Table 24. Modal Auxiliary Verbs 'May' and 'Must'

Modal	Negative	Meanings	Examples
may	may not	formal request, or permission	Q: *May I come* in, please? A: Yes, please come in. *May I be excused?*
		possibility in the future	I feel that *I may do* really well on the English exam. I feel pretty confident.
must	must not mustn't	obligation	He *must train* for the race if he has any chance to place well. *I mustn't drink* alcohol the night before a game. I'll let the team down.
		deduction	Q: Where is your homework? A: *I must have left* it at home.

Shall, Should and *Ought* (*to*) - Used in an *affirmative* and *negative statement,* or *interrogative* (shall and should mainly) with the words *I, you, we, they, he, she,* and *it,* or a *singular* or *plural noun phrase* as the *subject.*

Table 25. Modal Auxiliary Verbs 'Shall', 'Should' and 'Ought (to)'

Modal	Negative	Meanings	Examples
shall	shall not shan't	asking advice	What *shall I do* to make my classmates like me?
		suggestion	*Shall we eat* dinner before it's cold? *Shall I open* the door for you?
		future statement	All students *shall maintain* a 100% attendance record to pass my class.
should	should not shouldn't	offering advice	You *should practice* often to become talented at football. *Should you need* assistance, ask!
		expectation	My acceptance letter to university *should arrive* today.
ought (to)	ought not (to)	suggestion	You *ought to speak* at the Reunion.

Will - Used in an *affirmative* and *negative statement*, or *interrogative* with the words *I, you, we, they, he, she,* and *it*, or a *singular* or *plural noun phrase* as the *subject*.

Table 26. Modal Auxiliary Verb 'Will'

Modal	Negative	Meanings	Examples
will	will not won't	to insist	I **will not** *change* his mind.
		intention or promise	He **will** *take* an English exam today. She **will** *call* you as soon as she arrives!
		certainty in the future	I **will** *be* 50 next month.
		prediction	I doubt if **I'll** *climb* Mount Cook ever again.

Would - Used in an *affirmative* and *negative statement*, or *interrogative* with the words *I, you, we, they, he, she,* and *it*, or a *singular* or *plural noun phrase* as the *subject*. [the word *'would'* is often contracted to *'d*]

Table 27. Modal Auxiliary Verb 'Would'

Modal	Negative	Meanings	Examples
would or ~'d	would not wouldn't	habit performed in the past	When we were children, *we* **would** always *have* an annual family Reunion where we would play touch-football in the backyard.
		cautionary insistence	I **would** *suggest* you wear your life-jacket if you go out on the water!
		polite question	**Would** you *like* another plate of spaghetti and meatballs?
		preference	I **would** rather *be* inconspicuous.

QUOTE:

"The English language is nobody's special property. It is the property of the imagination: it is the property of the language itself."

Derek Walcott

❧ Regular and Irregular Verbs ❧

A *regular verb*, also known as a *weak verb*, is used to describe an *action*, *state* or *occurrence*. The form of a *main verb* can change by adding **-d** or **-ed**, or by changing **-y** to **-i** (if the *verb* ends in a consonant + **-y**) and then adding **-ed**, to create a *past simple tense* and *past participle* (A *verb* that functions as an *adjective*). Examples are:

Adding **-d** : *I save* money. ➡ *I sav**ed*** money.

Adding **-ed** : *I walk* to school. ➡ *I walk**ed*** to school.

Present Simple: *I study* English.

Past Simple: *I stud**ied*** English. (*I study* ➡ *I stud~~y~~* + *i* + **ed**)

Past Participle: *I have stud**ied*** English.

An *irregular verb*, also known as a *strong verb*, is used when the *past simple tense* and *past participle* cannot end with **-d** or **-ed**. Examples are:

Present Simple: *I eat* breakfast. (*I eat* + ~~ed~~)

Past Simple: *I ate* breakfast.

Past Participle: *I have **eaten*** breakfast.

There are about 200 common *irregular verbs* in the English language. Many others have become obsolescent or obsolete. Below is a sample list of the more common *irregular verbs* in use:

Table 28. Irregular Verbs (a more complete list is in the Appendix)

Base Form	Past Simple	Past Participle	Base Form	Past Simple	Past Participle
begin	began	begun	have	had	had
do	did	done	learn*	learnt learned	learnt learned
draw	drew	drawn	leave	left	left
dream*	dreamt dreamed	dreamt dreamed	ring	rang	rung
drive	drove	driven	rise	rose	risen
eat	ate	eaten	see	saw	seen
freeze	froze	frozen	sing	sang	sung
go	went	gone	swear	swore	sworn

*Some *verbs* can be both *regular* or *irregular*.

✤ Verb Tense and Future Time ✤

The *tense* expressed by a *verb* indicates *the time of the action* or *its state of being*. Technically, the English language has *two verb tenses* and a method to reference *future time:*

> **Present Tense**: A *verb tense* that expresses a *continual* or *habitual action, general truth / fact,* or *state of being*, with at least part of the element occurring in the *present time.*
>
> **Past Tense**: A *verb tense* that expresses a *continual* or *habitual action* or *state of being*, that occurred at a *definite time in the past*, which does NOT extend into the *present time.*
>
> **Future Time***: A form that expresses a *continual* or *habitual action* or *state of being* that has not yet begun.
>
> *The English language uses *modal auxiliaries, present and past tense forms*, and *adverbials of time*, to express an action that has not yet begun. Although there is no *future tense* in the English language, the correct *verb form 'future time'* is commonly referred to as a *future tense.*

Table 29. Verb Tense and Future Time Using the Verb 'Write'

	Simple	Continuous (Progressive)	Perfect	Perfect Continuous (Perfect Progressive)
Present	I write	I am writing	I have written	I have been writing
Past	I wrote	I was writing	I had written	I had been writing
Future	I will write	I will be writing	I will have written	I will have been writing

---

QUOTE:

"Arguments over grammar and style are often as fierce as those over Windows versus Mac OS, and as fruitless as Coca-Cola versus Pepsi and boxer underwear versus briefs."

Jack Lynch

Present Simple

Use the *present simple tense* to express *a situation, general truth / fact, a state of being* or *event* that exists now, at the time of speaking.

A situation, truth, fact, state or event

Past — Present — Future Time

Table 30. Structure for Present Simple Tense

subject pronoun, or noun phrase (or clause)	Affirmative *subject +* *main verb*		Negative *subject + aux. +* *not + main verb*		Interrogative *aux. + subject +* *main verb*		
	main verb		aux. + not	main verb	aux.	subject	main verb
I, you, we, they	admire crave enjoy live deliver etc.		do not don't	admire crave enjoy live deliver etc.	do	I, you, we, they	admire crave enjoy live deliver etc.
he, she, it	*main verb + s* ~ There are exceptions.		does not doesn't		does	he, she, it	
	orbits, eats, *etc.*						

Affirmatives:
    I <u>admire</u> volunteers.
    The Earth <u>orbits</u> around the Sun.

Negatives:
    She **does not** (**doesn't**) <u>crave</u> chocolate.
    They **do not** (**don't**) <u>enjoy</u> boating.

Interrogatives:
    Does Ralf <u>live</u> here?
    Do you <u>deliver</u> pizza?

Use the *present simple tense* to express *a single continual* or *habitual action*. At least part of the element must occur in the *present time*. *Frequency adverbs* are often used, such as: *often, daily, usually,* etc.

A single continual or habitual action

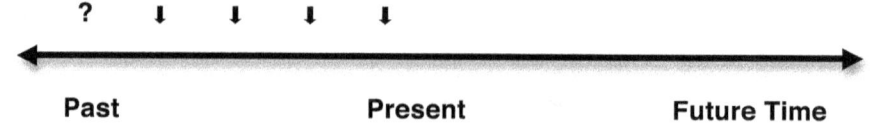

Affirmatives:

    I <u>entertain</u> guests often.

    He <u>paints</u> seascapes every day.

    We <u>shear</u> sheep every week.

Negatives:

    I **do not** (don't) <u>smoke</u> cigars often.

    She **does not** (doesn't) <u>practice</u> judo daily.

    They **do not** (don't) <u>go shopping</u> every week.

Interrogatives:

    Do you <u>recycle</u> newspapers weekly?

    Does she usually <u>knit</u> socks for all her grandchildren's gifts?

Table 31. Using 'be' Verbs as Main Verbs

	Subject	Main verb*	Neg.	Complement
Affirmative	I	am	—	twenty-one
	you, we, they	are	—	late
	he, she, it	is	—	smart
Negative	I	am	not	nervous
	you, we, they	are	not	early
	he, she, it	is	not	fat
Interrogative	am	I	—	right
	are	you, we, they	—	ready
	is	he, she, it	—	shrewd

*The **'be'** verb changes when it is used with another tense. For example: **'is'** and **'am'** → **'was'** or **'are'** → **'were'** for the *past tense*.

Past Simple

Use the *past simple tense* to express *a single event, action*, or *a series of completed events or actions* (1st, 2nd, 3rd, etc.) that began and ended at a particular time in the past.

The *past simple tense* can also be used to express *an extended duration of time that occurred in the past*, usually conveyed with words or phrases: *for* (~ 5-years, ~ fifty-years), *all* (~ day, ~ week, ~ year), etc.

single event or action
↓

←————————————————————————→

Past　　　　　　　　Present　　　　　　　　Future Time

Table 32. Structure for Past Simple Tense

subject pronoun, or noun phrase (or clause)	Affirmative subject + main verb + ed	Negative subject + aux. + not + main verb		Interrogative aux. + subject + main verb		
	main verb + ed	aux. + not	main verb	aux.	subject	main verb
I, you, we, they, he, she, it	played studied ate* ran* etc.	did not didn't	play study eat* run* etc.	did	I, you, we, they, he, she, it	play study eat* run* etc.
	*irregular verbs					

Affirmatives:

    I <u>played</u> football at noon, <u>took</u> a shower, then <u>went</u> home.

    They <u>ate</u> fish and chips last night.

Negative:

    My sister **did not** (didn't) <u>study</u> Spanish last Tuesday.

Interrogative:

    Did you <u>run</u> last week?

Future Simple

Use the *future simple* (*time*) to describe a *single event* or *action* that is planned and yet to occur.

single event or action

↓

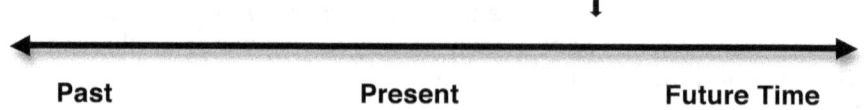

Past   Present   Future Time

Table 33. Structure for Future Simple Time

subject pronoun, or noun phrase (or clause)	Affirmative *subject + aux. + main verb*	Negative *subject + aux. + not + main verb*			Interrogative *aux. + subject + main verb*		
	aux.	aux. + not	main verb		aux.	subject	main verb
I, you, we, they, he, she, it	will (~'ll)	will not won't	call help coach eat play etc.		will	I, you, we, they, he, she, it	call help coach eat play etc.
I, we	shall	shan't			shall	I, we	
I	am (~'m) going to	am not going to			am	I (~ going to)	
you, we, they	are (~'re) going to	are not (aren't) going to			are	you, we, they (~ going to)	
he, she, it	is (~'s) going to	is not (isn't) going to			is	he, she, it (~ going to)	

Affirmative:

    *I **will** (shall) <u>call</u>* Henry next Tuesday.

Negative:

    *He **will not** (won't) <u>coach</u>* soccer later.

Interrogative:

    ***Will** you (shall we) <u>play</u>* football next Saturday?

Present Continuous

Use the *present continuous tense*, also known as the *present progressive tense*, to describe a *single event* or *action* that began in the recent past, has been continuous to the moment of speaking or writing, and is likely to end some time in the future.

The *present continuous tense* can also be used to *describe* or *express* a *general activity* that is ongoing, or planned, but not necessarily being done at this moment in time.

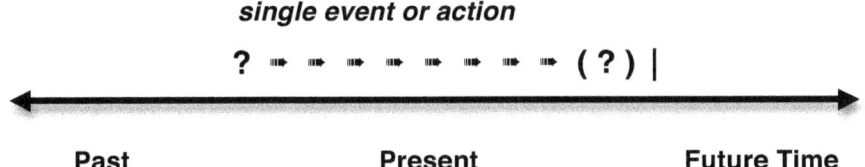

Past   Present   Future Time

Table 34. Structure for Present Continuous Tense

subject pronoun, or noun phrase (or clause)	Affirmative subject + aux. + present participle		Negative subject + aux. + not + present participle		Interrogative aux. + subject + present participle		
	aux.		aux. + not	present participle	aux.	subject	present participle
I	am (~'m)		am not	mov-ing	am	I	mov-ing
you, we, they	are (~'re)		are not aren't	hurt-ing los-ing	are	you, we, they	hurt-ing los-ing
he, she, it	is (~'s)		is not isn't	etc.	is	he, she, it	etc.

Affirmative:

    The Roberts **are** <u>moving</u> furniture now.

Negative:

    She **is not** (isn't) <u>hurting</u> anyone on purpose.

Interrogative:

    Are they <u>losing</u> weight for the upcoming boxing matches?

Ongoing:

    We **are** <u>learning</u> to ski this week. (time unknown)

Past Continuous

Use the *past continuous tense*, also known as the *past progressive tense*, to describe an *event* or *action* that was already in progress when it was interrupted by another *event* or *action*.

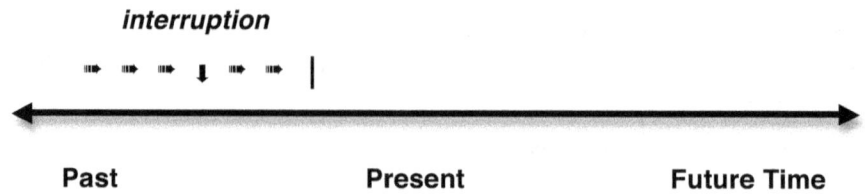

Table 35. Structure for Past Continuous Tense

subject pronoun, or noun phrase (or clause)	Affirmative *subject +* *aux. + present* *participle*	Negative *subject +* *aux. + not +* *present participle*		Interrogative *aux. +* *subject +* *present participle*		
	aux.	aux. + not	present participle	aux.	subject	present participle
I, he, she, it	was	was not wasn't	add-ing play-ing stack-ing etc.	was	I, he, she, it	add-ing play-ing stack-ing etc.
you, we	were	were not weren't		were	you, we, they	

Affirmatives:

    She **was** <u>knitting</u> sweaters for her two children.

    The apprentice cooks **were** <u>adding</u> milk and eggs to the cake recipe when the Sous-chef walked in.

Negatives:

    I **was not** (wasn't) <u>playing</u> football when the whistle blew.

    You **were not** (weren't) <u>making</u> tea when your dad arrived.

Interrogatives:

    Was he <u>barbecuing</u> sausages when his brother showed up?

    Were they <u>stacking</u> bricks when the supervisor called?

The *past continuous tense* can also be used in two or more parts of a sentence to show that the *event* or *action* was in progress simultaneously, but do not influence each other.

two simultaneous events or actions

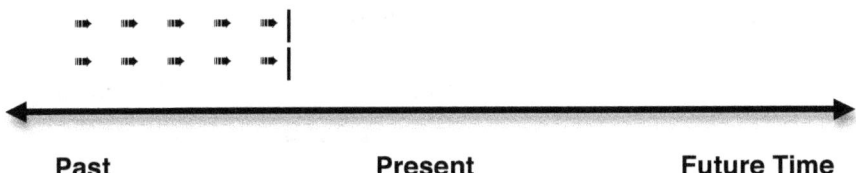

Past　　　　　　　　Present　　　　　　　　Future Time

Examples:

> John **was** *studying* British-American history while Jim **was** *reading* the newspaper.
>
> You **were** *eating* lunch while they **were** *shopping*.

The Humor of the English Language

1. I did not object to the object being lain at my feet.
2. The insurance claim was assessed as invalid for the invalid.
3. If teachers taught, why didn't preachers praught?
4. There was a row between the sea-scouts and the organizers on which row they should row in.
5. If you are close to the door then you should close it!
6. Does a buck's adrenaline increase when the does are close by?
7. A tailor and his sewer fell down a deep sewer.
8. Is it possible that a well-trained sow can sow seeds on the farm?
9. The dentist injected a number of shots into the patient's jaw, making his jaw number.

Future Continuous

Use the *future continuous* (*time*), also known as the *future progressive time*, to describe an *ongoing event* or *action* that will be happening at a particular time in the future. The *future continuous* (*time*) will contain either the verb phrase **'will be'** or **'shall be'** or **'going to be'** as well as a *present participle*.

ongoing event or action at a particular time

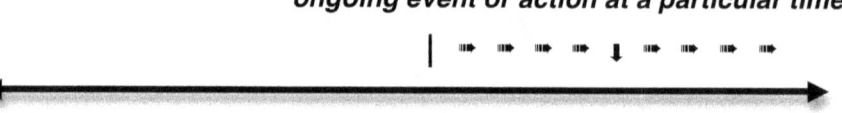

Past   Present   Future Time

Table 36. Structure for Future Continuous Time

subject pronoun, or noun phrase (or clause)	Affirmative *subject +* *aux. +* *aux. +* *present* *participle*	Negative *subject +* *aux. + not +* *aux. + present* *participle*			Interrogative *aux. +* *subject +* *aux. +* *present participle*			
	aux. + aux.	*aux. +* *not +* *aux.*	*present* *participle*	*aux.*	*subject*	*aux.*	*present* *participle*
I, you, we, they, he, she, it	will (~'ll) shall be	will / shall not be won't / shan't be	writ-ing clear-ing do-ing etc.	will shall	I, you, we, they, he, she, it	be	writ-ing clear-ing do-ing etc.

Affirmative:

*I **will be** writing* in my journal this afternoon.

Negatives:

*I **will not be** (won't be) clearing* the leaves from my garden when you return from work.

The girls **are not** (aren't) **going to be** doing dishes when their friends arrive.

Interrogative:

What **shall** you **be** doing when I return from holiday?

The *future continuous tense* can also be used to express *two or more events* or *actions* in the same sentence that are occurring simultaneously.

two simultaneous events or actions

Past   **Present**   **Future Time**

Examples:

> *John* **will be** <u>studying</u> fashion design while *Jim* **will be** <u>studying</u> the art of Ikebana.
>
> *I* am **going to be** <u>visiting</u> my doctor while *Jude* is **going to be** <u>attending</u> a job interview.

QUOTE:

"I don't know the rules of grammar ... If you're trying to persuade people to do something, or buy something, it seems to me you should use their language, the language they use every day, the language in which they think. We try to write in the vernacular."

David Ogilvy

Present Perfect

Use the *present perfect tense* to describe a *completed event* or *action* where the exact time is unknown.

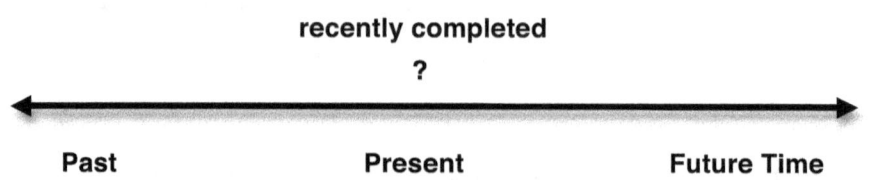

Table 37. Structure for Present Perfect Tense

subject pronoun, or noun phrase	Affirmative subject + aux. + past participle	Negative subject + aux. + not + past participle		Interrogative aux. + subject + past participle		
(or clause)	aux.	aux. + not	past participle	aux.	subject	past participle
I, you, we, they	have (~'ve)	have not haven't	seen (irregular) earn-ed	have	I, you, we, they	seen (irregular) earn-ed
he, she, it	has (~'s)	has not hasn't	eras-ed defus-ed etc.	has	he, she, it	eras-ed defus-ed etc.

Affirmative:

    We **have** just <u>seen</u> a child from Africa that we may adopt.

Negative:

    She **has not** (**hasn't**) <u>earned</u> our respect yet.

Interrogative:

    Have they <u>defused</u> the situation?

Use the *present perfect tense* to describe an *event* or *action* that began in the past where the exact time is unknown, and there is a connection to the present.

event or action still ongoing

Past **Present** **Future Time**

Examples:

I **have** <u>delivered</u> newspapers since I was young.

It **has** <u>hailed</u> off-and-on all week.

He **has** <u>eaten</u> spicy food since he was introduced to it some time ago.

Why the English Language is Difficult to Understand.

Quicksand works slowly, boxing rings are square, and a guinea-pig is neither from Guinea nor is it a pig, writers write, but fingers don't fing, and hammers don't ham.

There is no egg in eggplant or ham in hamburger; neither is there an apple nor pine in pineapple.

If a vegetarian eats vegetables, does a humanitarian eat humans?

We ship by truck, and send cargo by ship.

We have noses that run and feet that smell.

One goose, two geese. One moose two meese?

The bandage was wound around the wound.

The farm was used to produce produce.

Since there is no time like the present, he thought it was time to present the present.

Past Perfect

Use the *past perfect tense* to express a *completed event* or *action* that occurred before another *action* in the past.

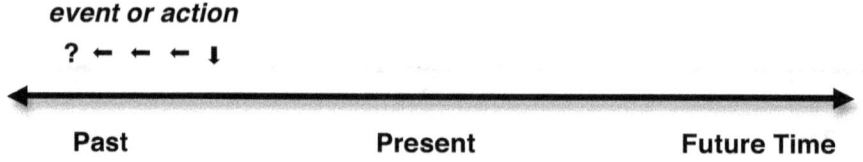

Table 38. Structure for Past Perfect Tense

subject pronoun, or noun phrase (or clause)	Affirmative subject + aux. + past participle	Negative subject + aux. + not + past participle		Interrogative aux. + subject + past participle		
	aux.	aux. + not	past participle	aux.	subject	past participle
I, you, we, they, he, she, it	had (~'d)	had not hadn't	learnt (irregular) edit-ed join-ed divert-ed etc.	had	I, you, we, they, he, she, it	learnt (irregular) edit-ed join-ed divert-ed etc.

Affirmatives:

> He **had** <u>learnt</u> the art of taxidermy from his grandfather before he opened his business.
>
> She **had** <u>edited</u> the book many times prior to publishing.

Negatives:

> They **had not** (hadn't) <u>joined</u> scouts.
>
> We **had not** (hadn't) <u>sought</u> reconciliation.

Interrogatives:

> **Had** they <u>diverted</u> funds before the scandal?
>
> **Had** he <u>bought</u> a car before he owned his Harley Davidson?

Future Perfect

Use the *future perfect* (*time*) to describe an *event* or *action* in the past from a viewpoint or position in the future.

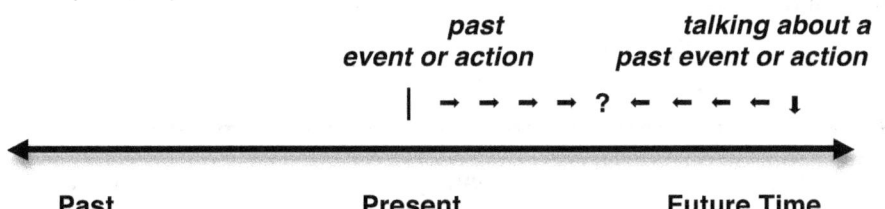

Table 39. Structure for Future Perfect Time

subject pronoun, or noun phrase (or clause)	Affirmative *subject + aux. + aux. + past participle*		Negative *subject + aux. + not + aux. + past participle*		Interrogative *aux. + subject + aux. + past participle*			
	aux. + aux.	aux. + not + aux.	past participle	aux.	subject	aux.	past participle
I, you, we, they, he, she, it	will (~'ll) shall have ~'ll've	will / shall not have won't / shan't have ~'ll not 've	eaten (irregular) finish-ed reward-ed shipp-ed etc.	will	I, you, we, they, he, she, it	have	eaten (irregular) finish-ed reward-ed shipp-ed etc.

Affirmatives:

    *I **will have** <u>eaten</u>* dinner prior to going to the movies.

    This time next week *I **will have** <u>finished</u>* painting my house.

Negative:

    *They **will not** (**won't**) **have** <u>shipped</u>* the package by Monday.

Interrogative:

    ***Will** you **have** <u>secured</u>* a seat by the time I arrive at the concert?

Present Perfect Continuous

Use the *present perfect continuous tense*, also known as the *present perfect progressive tense*, to express an *event* or *action* that has begun in the past and has recently completed, or has continued up to the present.

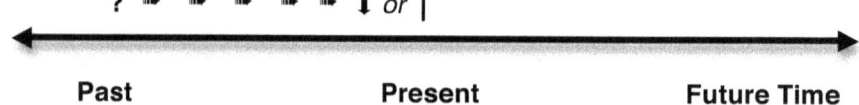

Table 40. Structure for Present Perfect Continuous Tense

subject pronoun, or noun phrase	Affirmative *subject + aux. + aux. + present participle*		Negative *subject + aux. + not + aux. + present participle*		Interrogative *aux. + subject + aux. + present participle*			
(or clause)	*aux. + aux.*		*aux. + not + aux.*	*present participle*	*aux.*	*subject*	*aux.*	*present participle*
I, you, we, they	have (~'ve) been		have not been haven't been	do-ing clean-ing tak-ing	have	I, you, we, they	been	do-ing clean-ing tak-ing
he, she, it	has (~'s) been		has not been hasn't been	rest-ing etc.	has	he, she, it		rest-ing etc.

Affirmatives:

    *I **have been** <u>co-writing</u>* a book. Now I can take a holiday.
    What ***have** you **been** <u>doing</u>*? *I **have been** <u>cleaning</u>* my car.

Negative:

    She seems depressed. I believe *she **has not been** (**hasn't been**) <u>taking</u>* her medication.

Interrogative:

    They look exhausted. ***Have** they **been** <u>resting</u>* well?

Use the *present perfect continuous tense* to express the *idea* that a situation is still in progress up until now.

situation in progress   *until now*

Past   Present   Future Time

Affirmatives:

I **have been** reading *A Tale of Two Cities* by Charles Dickens for several months.

He **has been** feeling really tired since working a double shift.

Negatives:

We **have not been** (haven't been) feeling one-hundred percent recently.

He **has not been** (hasn't been) studying since Monday.

Interrogatives:

Have *they* **been** waiting here for days?

Has *Janet* **been** designing her new home over the last few months?

QUOTE:

"Would mankind [humankind] be but contented without the continual use of that little but significant pronoun 'mine' or 'my own', with what luxurious delight might they revel in the property of others! ... But if envy makes me sicken at the sight of everything that is excellent out of my own [sic] possession, then will the sweetest food be sharp as vinegar, and every beauty will in my depraved eyes appear as deformity."

Sarah Fielding

Past Perfect Continuous

Use the *past perfect continuous tense*, also known as the *past perfect progressive tense*, to express an *event* or *action* that occurred over an extended period of time that had been happening before something else happened.

ongoing event / events or *action / actions*

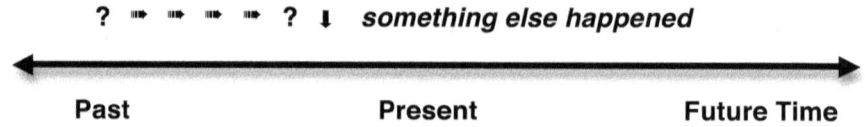

Table 41. Structure for Past Perfect Continuous Tense

subject pronoun, or noun phrase (or clause)	Affirmative subject + aux. + aux. + present participle		Negative subject + aux. + not + aux. + present participle		Interrogative aux. + subject + aux. + present participle			
	aux. + aux.		aux. + not + aux.	present participle	aux.	subject	aux.	present participle
I, you, we, they, he, she, it	had (~'d) been		had not been hadn't been	rid-ing fill-ing plann-ing etc.	had	I, you, we, they, he, she, it	been	rid-ing fill-ing plann-ing etc.

Affirmative:

    It **had been** <u>snowing</u> for hours.

Negative:

    Kathy **had not been** (hadn't been) <u>working</u> very long when major changes in organizational structure were implemented.

Interrogative:

    For how long **had** he **been** <u>planning</u> the festival when a city bylaw was introduced disallowing such festivals?

Future Perfect Continuous

Use the *future perfect continuous* (*time*), also known as the *future perfect progressive* (*time*), to express an *event* or *action* that is in progress and will continue sometime into the future, often prior to another.

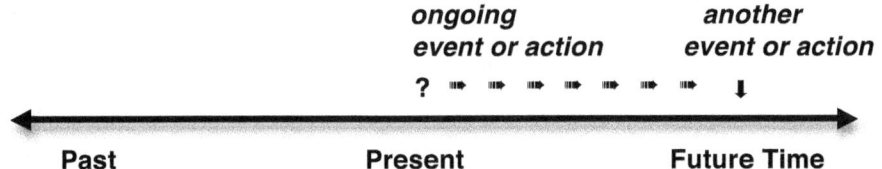

Table 42. Structure for Future Perfect Continuous Time

subject pronoun, or noun phrase (or clause)	Affirmative *subject + aux. + aux. + aux. + present participle*	Negative *subject + aux. + not + aux. + aux. + present participle*		Interrogative *aux. + subject + aux. + aux. + present participle*		
	aux. + aux. + aux.	aux. + not + aux. + aux.	present participle	aux.	subject	aux. + aux.	present participle
I, you, we, they, he, she, it	will (~'ll) shall have been ~'ll've been	will not / shall not have been won't / shan't have been	train-ing resourc-ing runn-ing etc.	will shall	I, you, we, they, he, she, it	have been	train-ing resourc-ing runn-ing etc.

Affirmative:

> He **will have been** <u>training</u> pilots for two-years by next month.

Negative:

> She **will not** (won't) **have been** <u>resourcing</u> companies with qualified staff for six months by the end of the year.

Interrogative:

> **Will** they **have been** <u>running</u> marathons by the time the first marathon starts this year?

✽ Subject Verb Agreement ✽

To identify the correct agreement between a *subject* and a *verb*, the *subject* must be identified. This can be achieved in two steps. First, find the *verb* (the action) [or state of being]. Second, find the *subject* by identifying who or what is performing that action. In the example below, the word *'rode'* reflects the action performed, so *'rode'* is the *verb*. The entity who *'rode'* the bike is *James*, so *James* is the *subject*.

> ***James*** (sub.) ***rode*** (v.) his bike down the road.
>
> **Hint:** If a word precedes the word 'of ' then it is most likely the subject, such as:
>
> ***The herd*** (sub.) <u>of</u> cows ***ate*** (v.) stored winter silage.

In this example the word *'ate'* is the *verb* (the action). It may seem like the *'cows'* are the *subject*, but this is not the case. It is the *'herd'* that performed the action, so *'herd'* is the subject.

The **'be'** verbs (non-action verbs) are: *be, am,* **are, is, was, were,** *being* and *been*. The **'be'** verbs reflect a *'state of being'*, rather than an action that is being performed. To choose the correct **'be'** verb, the *subject* must be identified. Examples are:

> ***He*** (sub.) ***is / was*** (v.) here.   ***They*** (sub.) ***are / were*** (v.) here.
> (not *He* ~~are / were~~...)   (not *They* ~~is / was~~...)
>
> ***The bushel*** (sub.) of apples ***is / was*** (v.) on the wagon.
> (*'The bushel'* is the *subject* not ~~apples [are]~~...)

Additional examples of specific *subject verb agreement* with the use of *indefinite pronouns* are:

Anyone, Everyone, Someone, ...

Indefinite pronouns such as *'anyone', 'anybody', 'someone', 'somebody', 'no one'* and *'nobody'* are *singular* [also sound *singular*] and therefore require an agreeable *singular verb*. The pronouns *everyone* and *everybody* are often seen to mean more than one person and sound plural, however, they are always treated as *singular*. Examples are:

> ***Somebody has*** <u>left</u> a handbag on the counter.
> ***Everyone has*** <u>completed</u> his or her assignment for this week.

Some *indefinite pronouns* such as *'some'* or *'all'*, can be either *singular* or *plural,* depending on whether they are referring to something that is either *countable* or *uncountable*. Examples are:

> ***Some*** of the beads ***are*** <u>missing</u>. (beads ➝ countable)
> ***All*** of the air ***is*** <u>polluted</u>. (air ➝ uncountable)

The indefinite pronoun *'none'* can be either *singular* or *plural*. If the *object* in the *prepositional phrase* is *singular*, then a *singular verb* is used. If the *object* in the *prepositional phrase* is *plural*, then a *plural verb* is used. Examples are:

None of the food *is* spicy. (food → singular)

None of the employees *are* complaining. (employees → plural)

None of the pilots *have* done their* annual training.

*The word their precludes the use of the *singular verb*.

The indefinite pronoun *'each'* [of] is *singular* and requires a *singular verb*; however, the word *'each'* is often followed by a *prepositional phrase* ending in a plural word, which often does cause confusion, such as:

Each of the boys **wears** a blue necktie with his uniform.

Together with, As well as, Along with

Phrases such as *'together with'*, *'as well as'*, and *'along with'* do not have the same meaning as the word *'and'*. In the example below, the phrase *'as well as'* modifies the preceding word *'student'*, but the phrase does not compound the *subjects,* as does the word *'and'*. Examples are:

The student, **as well as** his classmates, **is** going to a rugby game.

The student **and** his brothers **are** going to the basketball game.

Neither and Either

The indefinite pronouns *'neither'* (negative) and *'either'* (positive) almost always require *singular verbs*, even though they seem to be referring to two things. Examples are:

Do you want to eat or rest? **Neither** is what I really want to do.

Student: Teacher! Which textbook do you want me to open?

Teacher: **Either is** OK with me so long as you are studying.

Informally, the indefinite pronouns *'neither'* or *'either'*, when paired with the preposition *'of'*, [sometimes known as an of-pronoun], can optionally take either a *singular* or *plural verb* [this grammar rule is currently debatable]. However, the *pronoun* and *preposition* pairing must precede either a *plural pronoun* or a *plural noun phrase*. Examples are:

Neither of them **is (are)** studying.

Neither of the cows **has been (have been)** milked yet.

Either of the students **is (are)** welcome to attend.

Nor and Or

The conjunction *'or' does not conjoin*. When either *'nor'* or *'or'* is used, the *subject* closest to the *verb* determines the *singular* or *plural* state of the *verb*. Whether the *subject* comes before or after the *verb* doesn't matter; the proximity determines the usage. Examples are:

Either John <u>or</u> his **classmates** ← **are** <u>going</u> to sweep the floor.
Neither my classmates <u>nor</u> my **class-captain** ← **is** <u>going</u> to attend.
Are either → *my* **classmates** <u>or</u> my teacher responsible?
Neither my teacher <u>nor</u> my **classmates** ← **are** available!

There and Here

The adverbs (of place) *'there'* and *'here'* are never *subjects*. They are often used to construct expletive sentences. Find the subject in the sentence and then apply the agreeable verb. In the following, the subject follows the verb, but still determines the verb's numerical state:

There **are** <u>three reasons</u> (det. + plural subject) why this won't work.
There **is** <u>no reason</u> (det. + singular subject) for any change.

Verbs in the Present Tense

A *verb* in the *present tense* for a *singular subject*, such as *'he'*, *'she'*, and *'it'* (third-person), or any alternative to these, requires an *'s'* ending.

A *verb* in the *present tense* for a *plural subject*, such as *they*, *we*, or any alternative to these, doesn't have an *'s'* ending. Examples are:

He love**s** to study English every day!
They love to walk on the beach on hot Sunday afternoons.

Nouns Ending with 's'

Some *nouns* that end with the letter *'s'* are *plural* and require a *plural verb*. Examples are:

My **assets were** liquidated when bad times hit.

The average students' **grades have** <u>gone</u> up dramatically since last term.

Our **hearts go** out to all those who lost their lives and possessions during the devastating tsunami.

Some *nouns* that end with the letter *'s'* appear to be plural, but are really *singular* and require *singular verbs*. Examples are:

The ongoing news about the Economy **is** not so good.

Herpes is a dangerous viral disease affecting the skin or nervous system.

Fractional Expressions

Fractional expressions, such as: *'half of', 'part of', 'percentage of'*, or *'majority of'*, can either be *singular* or *plural*, depending on their meaning [This is also true for the words: *all, any, some, more,* and *most,* when they act as a subject.]. Furthermore, sums and products of mathematical processes are expressed as *singular* and require *singular verbs*. Examples are:

Some of the students **are** still not happy with their performance.

A large percentage of the senior class **is** <u>taking</u> their final exams today.

Two-fifths of the teachers **have** 20-years or more experience.

Half of the school **was** <u>destroyed</u> by the Earthquake.

Forty percent of the students **are** in favor of the new uniforms.

Sixty percent of the student body **is** in favor of a new English language department wing.

It's not that easy! **One plus one is** not always two.

Five times four **divided by two is** (or *equals*) ten.

The expression *'more than one'* is also expressed as *singular*, such as:

More than one student **has** <u>tried</u> to outsmart his teacher at one time or another; the emphasis is on 'tried'. You're not so unique!

Positive Verses Negative Subject

If a sentence compounds a *positive* and a *negative subject* and one is *plural*, the other *singular*, the *verb* should agree with the *positive subject*. Examples are:

The Judo team members, but not their coach, **have** <u>decided</u> to attend a professional match next week.

It is not the staff members, but **the principal**, who **decides** on major issues.

It was **the politician**, not his party's ideas, that **has** <u>provoked</u> the students to organize a sit-in.

PART FIVE — Adverbs (adv.)

Adverb Use

An *adverb* is a word that describes and clarifies a *verb*. An *adverb* can also *modify an adjective* or *another adverb*.

An *adverb modifies a verb*. Examples are:

John drove ***quickly***.

I ***almost*** fell asleep.

An *adverb* modifying an *adjective* usually precedes the *adjective*. Examples are:

John's English class was ***really*** great.

Japanese students are ***very*** clever!

An *adverb* modifying another *adverb* usually precedes the word it is modifying. Examples are:

John drove ***quite*** quickly up the street.

The answer you gave was ***really*** rather simple.

Adverb Types

There are five (5) main types of *adverbs*. These are: *degree, manner, place, frequency,* and *time.*

Adverbs of *degree*

These *adverbs* provide information on *how much* of something is done, such as:

almost, completely, deeply, entirely, fully, little, most, much, quite, rather, really, so, totally, too, very, etc.

Examples:

They were ***completely*** exhausted from three days of nonstop study.

We were ***totally*** prepared for the English exam.

Adverbs of *manner*

These *adverbs* provide information on *how* something happens or is done, such as:

carefully, enthusiastically, fast, gracefully, hard, how, impatiently, politely, quietly, slowly, so, stealthily, etc.

Examples:

I have (I've) noticed that my mom works **hard**.

John spoke **quietly** as he walked **slowly** past the sleeping bear.

Adverbs of *place*

These *adverbs* provide information on *where* something happened, happens, or may happen, such as:

about, above, behind, below, downstairs, far, here, indoors, near, outside, towards, there, where, etc.

Examples:

He ran **downstairs**, so he would be on-time.

I will meet you **outside** after the exam.

Adverbs of *frequency*

These *adverbs* provide information on *how often* that something happens, such as:

Definite: *annually, daily, hourly, nightly, yearly,* etc.

Indefinite: *always, generally, normally, occasionally, regularly, seldom, sometimes, usually,* etc.

Examples:

The school was moderated **annually**.

He **seldom** comes to school early.

Adverbs of *time*

These *adverbs* provide information on *when* something occurs, such as:

already, before, first, finally, late, now, previously, since, still, then, today, tomorrow, tonight, yesterday, yet, etc.

Examples:

Mary finished her English exam **first**.

I arrive **late** for most classes.

Other Uses

An *adverb* can also be used to:

Add or to limit:
> *also, either, else, neither, only, too, ...*

Reflect a viewpoint:
> *mentally, morally, officially, personally, strictly, ...*

Link ideas:
> *firstly, however, nevertheless, so, therefore, ...*

Reflect an opinion:
> *actually, fortunately, oddly, perhaps, strangely, surely, ...*

Adverb Intensifiers

An *adverb* can function as *an intensifier* reflecting a greater or lesser emphasis to something. These *intensifying adverbs* have three different functions. These are:

Emphasizer:
> Susan **really** doesn't believe she will pass her exam even though she studied all night.
>
> The English exam will be difficult, **for sure**!

Amplifier:
> The exam supervisor **completely** rejected her request for extra time.
>
> They **absolutely** refuse to give up on achieving high scores on my English exam.

Diminisher (to tone down or down-toner):
> John **almost** gave up studying English.
>
> I **somewhat** agree with you.

✤ Forming an Adverb ✤

An *adverb* can be formed in different ways. Here are a few examples:

1. By adding *-ly* to an *adjective*. Examples are:

   absolutely, anxiously, cheerfully, constantly, extremely, hardly, locally, occasionally, perfectly, positively, quickly, rarely, safely, usually, etc.

2. By adding *-ally* to an *adjective* ending with *-ic* :

academic → academically	athletic → athletically
automatic → automatically	dramatic → dramatically
drastic → drastically	fantastic → fantastically

3. By adding *-ly* to an *adjective* ending with *-al* :

accidental → accidentally	emotional → emotionally
geographical → geographically	traditional → traditionally
sentimental → sentimentally	national → nationally

4. If an *adjective* ends in a consonant **+ -y**, then change *-y* to *-ily* :

happy → happily	hungry → hungrily
lazy → lazily	lucky → luckily
noisy → noisily	speedy → speedily

5. If an *adjective* ends with *-le*, preceded by a consonant, then change *-e* to *-y* :

enjoyable → enjoyably	gentle → gently
fashionable → fashionably	incredible → incredibly
notable → notably	possible → possibly

6. If an *adjective* ends with *-le*, preceded by a vowel, then add *-ly* :

agile → agilely	sole → solely
vile → vilely	exception e.g.: whole → wholly

7. If an *adjective* ends with *-ue*, then change *-e* to *-ly* :

due → duly	true → truly

Note: There are some *adverbs* that do not end in *-ly* and there are some words that end in *-ly* that are not *adverbs*. For example:

   He drove **fast**.
   She was a *lovely* woman.
   I work with many *friendly* people.

✹ Adverb Placement ✹

An *adverb* can be placed in the following manner; however, an *adverb* is never placed between the *verb* and the *object*. Here are some examples:

At the beginning of a sentence, before the *subject:*

adverb + subject + verb (verb phrase) + ...

Unfortunately, we could not (couldn't) go to English language class as planned.

In the middle of a sentence between the *subject* and the *verb:*

subject + adverb + verb (verb phrase) + ...

John **frequently** passed exams with ease.

subject + 'be' verb + adverb + ...

Adam is **continually** showing up unannounced.

At the end of a sentence, after the *verb* or *object:*

subject + verb (verb phrase) + ... + adverb

He talks on his mobile phone **loudly**.

More than one *adverb* in a sentence:

subject + verb (verb phrase) + ... + adverb + ... + adverb

Casper studies English **diligently**, in the library, **daily**.

It is good practice to limit the use of *adverbs* to one or two per sentence. If more are used, then they should be used sparingly and be thoughtfully placed to maximize their impact, such as:

Consistently, every evening after eating his dinner, John **quietly** studies English **diligently** and **continuously** for hours.

Note: Caution. The overuse of *adverbs* [also true for the overuse of *adjectives*] may overwhelm the recipient and weaken the overall effect of the communication.

✹ Adverb Order ✹

Adverb order is as follows:

1. *degree*
2. *manner*
3. *place*
4. *frequency*
5. *time*

Conjunctive Adverbs

A *conjunctive adverb*, also known as a *connecting adverb*, is used as a connection word to link a deeper relationship between different clauses or sentences. These are words such as:

accordingly	*also*	*anyhow*
consequently	*furthermore*	*however*
moreover	*nevertheless*	*otherwise*
subsequently	*then*	*therefore*

There are several different *conjunctive adverb forms*. Here are a few examples:

1. When a *conjunctive adverb* is used at the beginning of a sentence, a *comma* is placed after the *adverb*, followed by the remaining sentence, such as:

    conjunctive adverb, + main clause

    The actual exam papers were not delivered in time. **Subsequently**, there will be no exam today.

2. When a *conjunctive adverb* is used between *two independent clauses*, a *semicolon* is required before the *adverb* with a *comma* following. Examples are:

    main clause; + conjunctive adverb, + main clause

    I want to go and play football; **however**, I need to study English first.

    I plan to wake up at 06:00; **then**, if the weather permits, I will go for a 25K run.

3. When a *conjunctive adverb* is placed within a *clause* as an interruption, then *commas* are placed around the *adverb*, to set it off and link the ideas within that and the previous sentence, such as:

    start of main clause, conjunctive adverb, + end of main clause

    The exam is over. I will**, nevertheless**, attempt to gain permission to take the exam tomorrow.

4. When a *conjunctive adverb* is placed at the end of a *clause* as a conclusion, then a *comma* is placed prior to the *adverb*:

    main clause, + conjunctive adverb

    After studying all night, Rick was too tired to eat breakfast. He did brush his teeth before going to work, **however**.

5. When a *conjunctive adverb* is placed as a weak break or conclusion, then it is unnecessary to use *commas*. Examples are:

> Jack called to say he would be late for work. The manager will **therefore** have to ask others to cover him until he shows up.

> Jack spilled paint all over his suit. Painting the house without coveralls was a mistake ***indeed***!

✽ Interrogative Adverbs ✽

An *Interrogative adverb* is usually used at the beginning of a *direct question*.

Note: In formal writing it is best to convert *indirect questions* into *direct questions* as follows:

> Explain to me how you came to that conclusion.
> ↓ ↓
> How did you come to that conclusion?

The four *interrogative adverbs* are:

how (degree or manner)   where (place)   when (time)
why (reason)

The interrogative adverb 'how' can be used in different ways. Here are a few examples:

Used with an *adverb*:

> **How** quickly can you come over?

Used with an *adjective*:

> **How** long is a piece of string?

Used with *much* and *many:*

> **How** much does an education cost?
> **How** many students are enrolled in next year's course?

Used to express, in what way, something *did* or *does* form or *happen*:

> **How** did you get to school this morning?
> **How** do you form a 'how' question?

PART SIX — Prepositions (prep.)

A *preposition* is a word that specifies concepts of *place, motion, direction,* and *time*. A *preposition* usually precedes a *noun, noun phrase* or *pronoun*. The structure is:

... + preposition + noun, noun phrase or pronoun

There are many *prepositions* in the English language. Here is a list of a few:

about	*above*	across	after
against	along	among	around
as	*at*	*before*	behind
below	between	beyond	*by (beside)*
down	*during*	except	*for*
from	*in*	inside	*into*
like	near	of	off
on	onto	opposite	outside
over	*past*	round	*since*
than	through	*to*	toward (s)
under	*until (till)*	up	upon
with	*within*	without	

The most commonly used *prepositions* are *at, in,* and *on*. These *prepositions* are divided into two main groupings, *place* or *time*. Examples of their usage are:

at:
>I will be *at* the office all day. (place)
>
>I cannot meet you *at* the moment. (point in time)

in:
>I performed *in* Auckland on New Year's day. (place)
>
>John F. Kennedy was assassinated *in* 1963. (point in time)

on:
>Put another shrimp *on* the Barbie! (place or position)
>
>Our family tradition is to eat pizza and watch a movie *on* Friday nights. We call this 'pizzovie' night! (point in time)

Note: Further information on *place* and *time prepositions* are discussed within their appropriate sections.

Here are some basic rules when applying *prepositions*. These are:

1. In most cases a *preposition* is followed by a *noun, noun phrase,* or *pronoun*. Examples are:

    John talked **to** Jim about the upcoming exam.

    The bank is **beside** the language school.

2. A *noun clause* can be the *object* of a *preposition*, such as:

    There is meaning **in** what you do!

3. A *preposition* may include two or more *nouns, noun phrases* or *pronouns* in the same sentence, such as:

    He owns homes **in** Auckland and Seattle.

4. A *preposition* is never followed by a *verb*. However, if a *verb* is used, it can only be a *gerund*, the **-ing** form of a *verb;* a verb in noun form, such as:

    I am keen **on** learning Thai cooking.

5. On occasion, a *preposition* is placed after the *noun, noun phrase* or *pronoun*, such as:

    This is *the student* I was speaking **of**?

6. Sometimes an *adverb* may be the *object*, such as:

    Your suit alterations will be done **by** then.

Although a *preposition* is usually placed before the *noun, noun phrase* or *pronoun*, they can also be positioned differently depending on the sentence structure, such as:

Active:

   My wife *has taken good care* **of** me.

Passive:

   The husband *has been well looked* **after**.

Question:

   What are you worrying **for**?

Comparison:

   He's attended more classes **than** I have.

Infinitive:

   These instructions are difficult **to** understand.

❋ Place, Space & Direction: (at, in, on...) ❋

A *place preposition* is used to describe the *place*, *space* or *direction* of a *noun, noun phrase* or *pronoun*. The most frequently used *place prepositions* in the English language are: *at, in,* and *on.*

at:
Used to indicate that something or someone is at a specific place.

...***at*** (the) church...   ...***at*** home...
...***at*** the airport...   ...***at*** the doctor's office...

In:
Used with a location to indicate a position within, or enclosed by an area or space.

...***in*** a town...   ...***in*** New Zealand...
...***in*** the park...   ...***in*** the room...

on:
Used to describe a location or position that is physically on top of a place.

...***on*** the Sunshine Coast...   ...***on*** a mountain...
...***on*** the table...   ... (eggs) ***on*** toast...

Table 43. Prepositions of Place, Space, Location, or Direction

Point or Place *at*	Inside a Space *in*	Surface or Within *on*
at the bus stop ***at*** the door ***at*** the front desk	***in*** Vancouver ***in*** a tree ***in*** the building	***on*** TV ***on*** the menu ***on*** a train
Prepositions	Categories	Examples
above	higher than	The fog rose ***above*** the lake.
across	the other side of	Use extreme caution when you walk ***across*** the road.
below	lower than	The duck dove ***below*** the water.
by or beside	near or next to	The bank is ***beside*** the cafe.
from	originate	Aren't Jack and Jill ***from*** here?
into	to enter	Please go ***into*** the garage and get my hammer!

✽ Time (at, in, on…) ✽

A *time preposition* is used to define *time*. The following table contains examples for some of the most frequently used *time prepositions* in the English language:

Table 44. Prepositions of Time

Precise Time *at*	Months, Years, etc. *in*	Days, Dates, etc. *on*
at 12 o'clock *at* 3 pm *at* lunchtime *at* bedtime *at* sunrise / sunset *at* the moment Let's meet *at* noon.	*in* December *in* (the) winter *in* the `60s *in* 1963 *in* the last century *in* my lifetime Call me *in* two days.	*on* Monday *on* (*at*) the weekend *on* Tuesdays *on* 21 November, 1963 *on* New Years *on* their birthdays You need to be *on* time.
Prepositions	Categories	Examples
after	later	I prefer that you talk to me *after* work.
before	ahead of previous	Can you meet Ruth and I *before* lunch? There are so many challenges *before* us!
between	separation	I can see you *between* one and two o'clock.
by	by the end of a particular time period	She promised to be here *by* the weekend.
during	position throughout	There should not be any talking *during* exams. He studied mathematics and science *during* the night.
for	duration period	I have not been to a movie *for* a long time. I have been studying *for* almost a year.

Prepositions	Categories	Examples
past	later than	Please meet Lenard and I at half ***past*** twelve.
since	past to present	The weather has been getting hotter and hotter ***since*** July.
to	before motion	All textbooks will be issued prior ***to*** class.
until ('til)	occurrence specified time	They all studied together ***until*** midnight.
within	period	Jude and I will be there ***within*** an hour!

⌘ Compound or Complex Prepositions ⌘

A *compound preposition*, also known as *complex preposition*, is formed with two or more words. This is sometimes referred to as *an idiom phrase*. Here are a few of them:

Two words:

according to	*apart from*	*because of*
due to	*except for*	*instead of*
out of	*prior to*	*where as*

Three or more words:

as far as	*as long as*	*as well as*
by means of	*for lack of*	*in addition to*
in front of	*on behalf of*	*on top of*
with regard to	*with respect to*	*with a view to*

QUOTE:

"When I read some of the rules for speaking and writing the English language correctly, I think any fool can make a rule, and every fool will mind it."

Henry David Thoreau

PART SEVEN — Conjunctions (conj.)

A *conjunction* is used to *link* or *join* phrases, *clauses*, or *two or more words together*, within the same sentence. There are two primary types of *conjunctions*: *coordinating* and *subordinating*, each type utilizing a different subgroup of *correlative* (*double*) *conjunctions*.

�֎ Coordinating Conjunctions ✶

A *coordinating conjunction* is used to *link* or *join phrases, clauses* or *words that are grammatically equal or similar*, in the following manner:

    phrase + *coordinating conj.* + phrase

    clause + *coordinating conj.* + clause

    word + *coordinating conj.* + word

There are seven (7) main *coordinating conjunctions* in the English language. The most commonly used are: *and, or,* and *but*. The other four are: *for, nor, so,* and *yet*. Here are examples of their usage:

    and:

        Phrases: Would you like a cappuccino **and** biscotto?

        Clauses: Students of all ages arrived at school, **and** the daily routine began.

        Words: I study both English **and** Japanese.

    or:

        Phrases: You can wear a suit **or** semi-formal attire.

        Clauses: Would you like to drive by car, **or** would you prefer to take a taxi?

        Words: I recommend that you visit the UNESCO World Heritage Site Historic Monuments of Ancient Kyoto (Kyoto, Uji and Otsu Cities) once **or** twice.

    but:

        Phrases: The English language school in Auckland city is small **but** very credible.

        Clauses: Many are called, **but** few are chosen.

The other main *coordinating conjunctions* are:

    for:

        Mr. John Jones was elected as the president, **for** he was the right person for the job.

nor:
> I don't believe the Prime-Minister is right, **nor** do I think he ever will be.

so:
> He has to study for the exam tonight, **so** he cannot make it to the party.

yet:
> John said he was too sick to go to school, **yet** he was well enough to want to go to the movies.

Here are a few rules when using *coordinating conjunctions*:

1. A *coordinating conjunction* will always be placed between the *phrases, clauses* or *words* they link or join.

2. When a *coordinating conjunction* joins *clauses*, a *comma* at the end of the first clause is used for most sentences (see rule #3. exception below):

   > I want to become an international business person, so I want to learn the English language.

3. If the *coordinating conjunction* joins *clauses* that are grammatically equal, similar and just a few brief words, a comma is not essential. Furthermore, part of the second clause is omitted, a comma is not required. Examples are:

   > He was hungry **so** he ate.
   > Sophia rushed to work **and** (~~she~~) was on time.

4. When the last *coordinating conjunction* used in a list is *'and'*, a *comma* is optional:

   > My favorite foods are macaroni and cheese, pizza, hot-dogs **and** pickles.

❈ Subordinating Conjunctions ❈

A *subordinating conjunction* is used to link or join a *subordinate dependent clause* to a *main clause*, often to compare or show contrast.

There are several *subordinating conjunctions* in the English language. Here are three common examples:

although:
> They all went paragliding **although** no one had experience.

since:
> My classmates have decided to tour New Zealand together **since** no one had any other plans.

until:
> Please remain seated **until** I release you all.

Here are some other *subordinating conjunctions:*

after	as	as if	as though
as long as	as soon as	if	if only
in order that	in case	lest	once
now that	only if	provided that	so that
so long as	when	where	whereas
wherever	while	who	why

Here are a few rules when using *subordinating conjunctions*:

1. A *subordinating conjunction* is placed between a *main clause* and *subordinate dependent clause.* Examples are:

    John attended The University of British Columbia **while** his sister went to Oxford.

    I will go to the shopping mall **once** my mom gives me my allowance.

2. A *subordinate clause* is always dependent on a *main clause*.

3. A *subordinate clause* can often precede an *independent clause:*

    While I was sleeping, my mother cooked dinner.

    Although it was cold outside, Veronica went swimming.

✾ Correlative or Double Conjunctions ✾

Correlative conjunctions, also known as a *double conjunctions*, are a subgroup of both *coordinating* and *subordinating conjunctions*. They are always used in pairs to *link* or *join* equivalent grammatical elements (parts) in a sentence.

Here are some examples of *coordinating correlative (double) conjunctions:*

both...and... :

Both New Zealand **and** South Africa are rugby nations.

either...or... :

Either Jackson **or** Thompson will win the election.

neither...nor... :

I **neither** like **nor** dislike golf.

not only...but also... :

Jim **not only** scored the winning goal **but** (~~he~~) **also** was selected as the most valuable player.

82

Here are some examples of *subordinating correlative (double) conjunctions:*

whether...or... :

Robert has not decided **whether** to go to the soccer **or** stay home and rest.

if...then... :

If it rains tomorrow morning **then** I will need to take my umbrella with me to work.

so...that... :

They were **so** excited **that** their new baseball uniforms had arrived.

Phoney Phonetics *(slightly modified)*.

One reason why I cannot spell, although I learned the rules quite well, is that some words like *coup* and *through* sound just like *threw* and *flue* and *who*; when *oo* is never spelled the same, the *duice* becomes a guessing game; and then I ponder over *though*, is it spelled *so*, or *throw*, or *beau*, and *bough* is never *bow*, it's *bow*, I mean the *bow* that sounds like *plow*, and not the *bow* that sounds like *row* - the *row* that is pronounced like *roe*.

I wonder, too, why *rough* and *tough*, that sound the same as *gruff* and *muff*, are spelled like *bough* and *though*, for they are both pronounced a different way.

And why can't I spell *trough* and *cough* the same as I do *scoff* and *golf*?

Why isn't *drought* spelled just like *route*, or *doubt* or *pout* or *sauerkraut*?

When words all sound so much the same to change the spelling seems a shame.

There is no sense - see sound like *cents* - in making such a difference between the sight and sound of words; each spelling rule that undergirds the way a word should look will fail, and often prove to no avail, because exceptions will negate, the truth of what the rule may state; so though I try, I still despair and moan and mutter "It's not fair that I'm held up to ridicule and made to look like such a fool when it's the spelling that's at fault.

Let's call this nonsense to a halt.

Attributed to Vivian Buchan, NEA Journal 1966/67, USA, published in Spelling Progress Bulletin Spring 1966, p6.

PART EIGHT — Interjections (interj.)

An *interjection* is a word used to *express* or *convey* a strong sudden *emotion, sentiment,* or *abrupt remark.* Some *interjections* are:

>disgust   enthusiasm   excitement   surprise

An *interjection* is not grammatically related to any other part of a sentence. It is attached to and is usually followed by a *comma* or an *exclamation mark*.

Interjections are not usually used in formal writing, except in *direct quotations, plays,* or *scripts.*

Table 45. Interjections

Interjections	Meanings	Examples
ah	complaint, dislike, joy, pain, pity, pleasure, realization, resignation, surprise	*Ah,* I understand now! *Ah,* that feels good! *Ah!* I don't believe a single word you're saying!
alas	concern, pity, sorrow	*Alas!* The queen has passed.
bugger	imply dissatisfaction	*Bugger* , I lost my keys again!
dear me	distress, pity, surprise, sympathy	*Dear me!* That didn't happen to her did it?
eh	doubt, surprise	*Eh!* I don't believe you!
hello	elation, surprise, wonder	*Hello*---what's going on here? *Hello*---am I glad to see you!
hey	to call attention to, pleasure, surprise, bewilderment	*Hey,* that's great! *Hey!* Get out-ta [sic] here!
hmm or h'm	doubt, hesitation, perplexity, puzzled	*H'm,* I'm not so sure about that!
Jeepers (creepers)	frustration, emotion, surprise	*Jeepers (~ creepers)!* Did that really happen to you?
ooh or oh no	disapprobation, pain, surprise, joy	*Oh no!* I hope it's not true! *Ooh,* is that right?
ouch / ow	dismay, pain	*Ouch!* That really hurts!
ugh	disgust, horror	*Ugh,* this coffee is bitter!

CHAPTER TWO:
PUNCTUATION GUIDE

ENGLISH LANGUAGE PUNCTUATION

ACCEPTABLE USAGE

In written English, punctuation marks are used within sentences to remove uncertainty of meaning, or intention. Here is an example of two sentences with the same number of words and same word order, but differing punctuation, giving each sentence a different meaning:

The man ate and sang an hour after his head was cut off.
The man ate and sang; an hour after, his head was cut off.

Terminating Marks (.) (!) (?) (‽)

In the current written English language, there are only four *terminating marks* used to end a sentence. These are:

1. A period or full stop (.),
2. An exclamation mark (!),
3. A question mark (?), and
4. An interrobang or interabang (‽).

Period or Full Stop (.)

A *period* (.) [American grammatical terminology] or a *full stop* (.) [British grammatical terminology] is used to end all sentences other than emphasized statements where an *exclamation mark* is used (!), for questions where a *question mark* is used (?), or for emphasized questions where a *interrobang* is used (‽).

A *period* (or *full stop*) goes at the end of a sentence or inside a *closing quotation mark*, such as:

    Today is Monday.   He said, "I am hungry."

A *period* (or *full stop*) is used to designate an ordered list when coupled with numbers, the alphabet, or Roman numerals. Examples are:

1.	A.	a.	i.
2.	B.	b.	ii.
3.	C.	c.	iii.

A *period* (or *full stop*) is used to terminate an abbreviation:

Mr.	Mrs.	Miss.	Rev.
etc.	e.g.	i.e.	R.S.V.P.

A *period* (or *full stop*) is used at the end of an indirect quotation, such as:

    John asked if it rained yesterday.

A *period* (or *full stop*) is used with some name titles. Examples are:

    Dr. Thomas Julian…   Cpt. James Kirk…

Exclamation Mark (!)

An *exclamation mark* is used to emphasize a statement, or to express a sudden forceful emotion, plea, or cry. Examples are:

    Do not move or I will shoot!   Wow!
    I said be quiet!   Nonsense!

Question Mark (?)

A *question mark* is used to end a direct question that requires a response, such as:

    May I borrow a pen?

An enclosed *question mark* (?) is also used to indicate uncertainty or doubt by experts, NOT for use in general practice to indicate a lack of knowledge. An example of the correct usage is as follows:

    Joan of Arc, 1412 (?) – 30 May, 1431, is considered a French heroine and Catholic saint.

If a *question mark* is required at the end of a quote that is within *quotation marks*, then the *question mark* is placed inside the *quotation marks*, such as:

    John asked, "Where are my keys?"

If a *question mark* is required at the end of a sentence where a quotation is used, then the *question mark* is placed outside the *quotation marks*, such as:

Was John right when he said, "I am the luckiest man alive"?

In a question sentence, which also includes a question within *quotation marks*, use only one *question mark*, as follows:

Did John say, "Where are my keys?"

Note: Grammar rules dictate that only one *terminating mark* can be used in a sentence. However, there is an informal exception to this rule. Grammatically speaking, an exclamatory question <u>should not</u> use both a terminating *exclamation mark* (!) and a terminating *question mark* (?) at the same time. The following example is strictly for **informal** purposes:

An *exclamation mark* with a *question mark* at the end of the same sentence; are you kidding !?

The only formal solution to the simultaneous combining of a *terminating exclamation mark* (!) with a *terminating question mark* (?), at the conclusion of an exclamatory question, is the use of an *interrobang* (‽).

Interrobang (‽)

In formal writing, the *interrobang* [interabang] (‽) is used to ask a question emphasizing excitement, disbelief, or to ask a rhetorical question. Examples are:

You said what to her‽

She's pregnant again‽

✿ Ellipsis (...) ✿

An *ellipsis* (...), three periods in a row, is used to indicate the omission of a word, words, or a sentence or sentences in a quote. Examples are:

"I say to you today, my friends, so even though we face the difficulties of today and tomorrow, ...

I have a dream that one day this nation will rise up [sic] and live out the true meaning of its creed...

I have a dream that my four little children will one day live in a nation where they will not be judged by the color of their skin, but by the content of their character.

I have a dream today."

Martin Luther King, Jr.

If an omission occurs after a sentence, the three periods (...) are added after the termination period, such as:

"Twinkle, twinkle, little star. ...like a diamond in the sky."

✾ Comma (,) ✾

A *comma* is used to separate parts of a sentence into logical elements, helping to clarify the meaning of a sentence. A *comma* is generally understood to be a rest in a sentence, a micro-pause, or a place to take a quick shallow breath.

Here are several guidelines for using a *comma* effectively:

Distinguishing Parenthetical Elements

Use a *comma* to separate or distinguish a *parenthetical element* within a sentence. A *parenthetical element,* also referred to as *added information*, is any part of a sentence that can be removed without changing the real meaning of the remaining sentence. Examples are:

John F. Kennedy, the Thirty-fifth President of the United States of America, was assassinated in 1963.

Aung San Suu Kyi, after 15 of the 21 years of house arrest from July 20, 1989 until her release on 13 November 2010, was freed.

Note: *Parentheses* are sometimes used to reduce the importance of *parenthetical information*, such as:

Mr. Jones almost 40-year attendance record (with the exception of one day last June) has been exemplary.

Dashes are sometimes used to emphasize the importance of *parenthetical information*, such as:

Mr. Jones' almost 40-year attendance record—with not one recorded incident of lateness—has been exemplary.

As a general rule, set off *parenthetical information* with *commas*.

Separating Items in a Series

Use a *comma* to separate *words, phrases,* or *clauses* that appear in a series of three or more. The final item should have the *coordinating conjunction 'and'* placed before it. However, in the fourth example below, the word *'and'* is used with words that are inseparable:

1. I love to eat hamburgers, french-fries, onion-rings **and** apple pie.
2. I enjoy playing baseball at the park, taking long walks on the beach, hiking in the summer **and** swimming in the ocean.
3. My favorite sports are rugby, golf, soccer, yachting **and** fishing.
4. My favorite foods are macaroni **and** cheese **and** fish **and** chips.

The *'and'* between the word *'macaroni'* and the word *'cheese',* is placed to facilitate a link between two inseparable words, within the context of *'macaroni and cheese'* [to reflect one item or entity]. If macaroni, cheese, pizza, hot-dogs and pickles were expressed, then (in contrast) the meaning would change. In the fourth example, there are two items, and in the example inserted within this paragraph, there are five.

Serial (Oxford or Harvard) Comma

Use a *Serial Comma,* also known as a *Oxford, Harvard* or *Series Comma,* before the word *'and'* or *'or'* at the end of a sentence that contains a series of separate words, phrases, or clauses that appear in a series of three or more, such as:

My favorite hobbies are hiking, camping, fishing, and hunting.

Note: There is ongoing debate over the use of such a *comma.* Generally speaking, the *coordinating conjunctions 'and'* or *'or'* replace a *comma,* so some 'grammar experts' claim that the use of a *comma* coupled with the word *'and'* or *'or'* is redundant; however, if an *Serial Comma* can be used to prevent confusion, then common sense should prevail.

Introductory Phrase or Adverb Clause

Use a *comma* after an *introductory phrase* or *adverb clause* that precedes the subject of the sentence. Examples are:

An Introductory phrase:

Staring up at Mount Everest for the first time, he suddenly realized how insignificant he was.

An Adverb clause:

If the next two nights are sellouts, the concert schedule will be extended.

Setting Off Interruptions

Use a *pair of commas* to set off *words, phrases,* or *clauses* that interrupt a sentence. Examples are:

> Success, for the most part, is the application of a positive attitude.

> The Weather channel stated that the weather this week, I hope, will be absolutely fantastic.

However, be careful not to directly affect the essential meaning of the sentence by adding these elements.

Separating Dialog and Non-dialog Text

A *hyphen*, or *hyphens*, are used to *separate dialog* and *non-dialog text*, using introductory words. Here are a few of many, which can take different speech forms:

ask	*assert*	*boast*	*charge*
claim	*comment*	*continue*	*debate*
demand	*exclaim*	*hint*	*inform*
plead	*protest*	*said*	*write*

When a quote follows an introductory word, the *comma* is placed after the introductory word, a space is added, then an open *quotation mark* used, followed by the quote with the first letter capitalized; unless an *ellipsis* (...) is used to start the quote. Examples are:

> Martin Luther King, Jr. has become famous for the words in a speech he gave in which he said, "I have a dream today."

> *or*

> Martin Luther King, Jr. expressed hope when he said, "...my four little children will one day live in a nation where they will not be judged by the color of their skin... I have a dream today."

When an introductory word follows a quote, the *comma* is placed after the final word of the quote, directly followed by a closing *quotation mark*, a space, and then the introductory word, such as:

> "I have a dream today," said Martin Luther King, Jr. as he addressed the masses.

When introductory words are within a quote the correct punctuation will be as follows:

"...my four little children," said Martin Luther King, Jr., "will one day live in a nation where they will not be judged by the color of their skin... I have a dream today."

When an introductory and non-quote words are used before and after the quote the correct punctuation will be as follows:

Martin Luther King, Jr. said, "I have a dream today," as crowds of people listened.

Before a Coordinating Conjunction

A *coordinating conjunction* provides a connection between two similarly constructed and / or syntactically equal *words, phrases,* or *clauses* within a sentence. Examples of such words are:

| *for* | *and* | *nor* | *but* |
| *or* | *yet* | *so* | |

A *comma*, followed by one space, is placed before the *coordinating conjunction*. Examples are:

Jane screamed loudly, **for** she could no longer tolerate the pain.

To avoid being caught by police, Tom agreed to take the first watch, **and** Jim promised to relieve him within an hour.

Tom will never attempt bungee-jump, **nor** will he sky drive.

Jane dislikes running and swimming, **but** loves hiking.

I have a strong feeling it will rain today, **or** maybe it won't.

Jane is an extremely hyperactive individual, **yet** she will spend several hours watching a professional chess match.

Jim is unable to come to the party, **so** let's take the party to him.

The use of a *comma* before the *coordinating conjunction 'and'* or *'or'* is generally accepted as optional (see Serial Comma).

Separating Date Elements

Use a *comma* to separate the date from the year (American written dates only). Examples are:

January 26, 2012   (American)

26 January 2012   (British)

Use a *comma* to separate the day from the date. Examples are:

Tuesday, June 12, 2012 (American)

Tuesday, 12 June 2012 (British)

Within a sentence, use a *comma* on both sides of the year in a full American date (day, month with date, and year) and only on the right side of the year for a British date (day, date with month and year). Examples are:

On Friday, March 29, 2012, my Mom will have a birthday. (American)

On Friday, 29 March 2012, my Mom will have a birthday. (British)

Note: A *comma* is not used for two date elements, such as:

J. F. Kennedy's assassination in November 1963 is a moment in time many Americans are unwilling to forget.

Separating Number Elements

Use a *comma* in numbers of more than three digits, from right to left, as a thousands' separator. Examples are:

He had $12,527 in his bank account.

There were 57,653 people at the Rugby World Cup final.

Common exceptions include, but are not limited to this list:

1. Some countries (currency may differ),
2. Only use a *comma* in years of five digits or more, such as in 12,500 BC,
3. Street numbers may not use a *comma*, and
4. Page numbers.

Note: There may be many others. Self-study will be necessary.

Use a *comma* to separate related written measurements, such as:

The heavyweight boxer was six-feet, two-inches tall, and at weigh-in 180 pounds, 6 ounces.

Use a *comma* to separate elements in a play, such as:

Act III, Scene II, "Friends, Romans, countrymen, lend me your ears; I come to bury Caesar, not to praise him."

Within Names, Places, and Addresses

Use a *comma* to separate people's names and their academic degrees, such as:

David Alexandra, MD, will speak at the conference.

Use a *comma* between a name when a surname comes before a first, such as:

Kennedy, John F. was assassinated in November 1963.

Use a *comma* to separate place names with the smallest unit first, such as:

John lives on 12 Oaks Road, New York city, New York State, USA.

or, in a mailing address:

John Jones
2347A 12 Oaks Road,
New York, N.Y.,
U.S.A.

✂ Colon (:) ✂

A *colon* is usually used in conjunction with the preceding word and words. Examples are:

as follows: are: as: is:

A *colon* is used prior to a numbered list, a summarized list (within a sentence), or an indirect quote. Examples are:

A list:

My favorite pets are:

1. dogs,
2. horses, and
3. snakes.

A summarized list:

Before we depart we must achieve the following: catch the shark, tag it, and then release it unharmed.

An indirect quote:

...as Khalil Gibran wrote: and in much of your talking, thinking is half murdered.

A *colon* can be used to dramatically emphasize a single word or phrase, such as:

> There was only one choice left to make: resign!

A *colon* is used to divide a primary division from a secondary division. Examples are:

> Religious books:
>
>> The shortest verse in the King James version of the Christian Holy Bible is, John 11:35 "Jesus Wept."
>>
>> In the Holy Quran the shortest verse is 55:64 " ن ‌ان‌تمامدم. "
>
> Time:
>> 09:15   12:25   18:30

The use of *capitalization* or *lower-case* after a *colon* varies. In British English the word following the *colon* is in lower-case unless it is a proper noun, an acronym, or if it is normally *capitalized* for some other reason. In American English the word following a *colon* is *capitalized* only if it begins an *independent clause*.

✼ Semicolon (;) ✼

The *semicolon* is used to join an *independent clause* that is closely related in meaning. Examples are:

> Reducing fat in your diet will decrease the chances of heart disease; regular exercise is also important.
>
> **Note**: Generally speaking, use a *semicolon* only where a period could also be used.

The *semicolon* is also used to separate word groupings, such as:

> The New Zealand All-blacks battled the South African Springbok for 80-minutes of pure rugby, all players were tired, bruised, and exhausted; it was pride, passion, and the reward of victory that kept them all going.

✼ Dash (—) or (--), and Swung Dash (~) ✼

A *dash* is used to *emphasize, support,* or *explain,* and / or to *note a sharp change in thought*. Examples are:

Emphasis:

The concert was exciting—a fantastic show.
She is beautiful--a knockout.

Support or explain:

The Color Purple (1985) directed by Steven Spielberg—the first of several movies starring Oprah Gail Winfrey—is a classic.

President J. F. Kennedy--assassinated on November 22, 1963 (aged 46)--was sworn in as the 35th President of The United States of America at noon on January 20, 1961.

A sharp change in thought:

I'm sure Janet will go to the movies with you—I don't think she would say no.

A *dash* can also be used to express *hesitation* when writing, usually preceded with a word that reflects that a person is pondering the next idea. Examples are:

I mean:

I'm not sure if I want to go fishing, I mean—what if a big storm rolls in and we can't get back to shore?

I think:

Let's drive all night to Vegas. I think—no—I know we can make it before daylight, if we rotate drivers.

Maybe:

She said she would be here at 5 o'clock—maybe something has happened to her.

Um or ah:

John: Why are you late for work?
Jane: Um—Ah—I was kidnapped by aliens.

A *swung dash* is used to separate alternatives or indicate approximates. In dictionaries, a *swung dash* is frequently used to substitute a term being defined. For example, the word *'henceforth'* [(adv.) from this time forth; from now on], might be substituted with a *swung dash* in the following way:

"~ he will be known as *The Duke of York*."

Hyphen (-)

Between Compound Words

A *hyphen* is used between the individual parts of *compound words* to act as one idea. Examples are:

Between two *nouns:*

Christopher Neil, Bob Dylan, Amy Winehouse, and Lady Gaga are or were *singer-songwriters*.

You can buy milk at the *corner-store*.

Between two *adjectives* placed before a *noun:*

It is much more expensive to buy a *first-class* ticket.
He has a *care-free* attitude.

Between two *verbs:*

You need to *dry-clean* your pants before the next meeting

The plane had to *crash-land*.

Between an *adjective* and a *noun:*

I bought a *loose-leaf* binder at the shop.
I attended an *open-air* concert.

Between a *noun* and a *verb:*

It was *back-breaking* work.
I was *hand-picked* to attend the seminar   .

Two Words Linked by a Preposition

Sometimes two or more words are linked by *prepositions* with *hyphens*. Examples are:

She is my *sister-in-law*.   It is true *as-a-matter-of-fact*!
He is really a *down-to-earth* person.   I had the *right-of-way*.

Spelt Numbers and Cardinals

A *hyphen* is used between *spelt numbers* and between a *spelt number* and a *cardinal*. Examples are:

I have collected *twenty-three vintage-cars* over *thirty-three* years.

Less than *one-forth* of homes are adequately insulated.

Words with a Prefix

A *hyphen* is used after a *prefix*. Examples are:

The *prefix 'anti-'* expresses opposition to (or being against) the root word that adjoins it:

I operated an **anti-***aircraft* gun during WWII.

The **anti-***crime* unit hit with force.

The *prefix 'by-'* suggests that something has two, is doubled, or repeated or is secondary to the root word and is sometimes *hyphenated*. Examples are:

A **by-***product* of corn is organic fuel.

The city's **by-***law* states no dogs on any beach.

But not as in:

The city bypass is almost complete.

Let bygones be bygones.

The *prefix 'co-'* is used if the root word, usually a *verb* or it's *noun* derivative, begins with the letter *'o'* or with a *noun* to denote joint participation. Examples are:

The charity held a **co-***operative* fundraiser .

I need a **co-***ordinator* for the International Student Services position filled by Thursday next week.

or

My husband is a great **co-**driver on long journeys.

It is rare that a **co-***star* is paid more than the star .

The *prefix 'counter'* is used *'speak out'* or to *'act in opposition to'* something. Examples are:

The 10th Mountain Division planned a **counter-***attack*.

Arguing with a deadline looming can be **counter-***productive*.

But not as in:

The painting is a counterfeit.

It was necessary to counteract their action.

The *prefix 'ex-'* is used to express a former state to the root word. Examples are:

He is my **ex-***husband*.

Should I hire an **ex-***convict*?

97

The *prefix 'in-'* expresses an inclusion within *space, time* or *circumstances*. In most cases a hyphen is not used, but is used as in these examples:

    I want to hire **in**-*house*.

    I will have surgery at the **in**-*patient* clinic.

    But not as in:

        The lovers were **in**separable.   Are they **in**sane?

The *prefix 'non-'* reflects that there is a *'lesser value to'* or *'a lack of'* in relation to the root word. Examples are:

    I prefer **non**-*alcoholic* drinks.

    All **non**-*essential* workers were asked to go home.

The *prefix 're-'* (to do again) is used if the root word begins with the letter **'e'**. Examples are:

    It was necessary to **re**-*edit* the book prior to publishing after new information was found.

    I had to **re**-*establish* the restaurant after years of neglect.

The *prefix 're-'* is also used when forming a compound word, Not using a hyphen may change the words meaning, as in:

recover	**re**-*cover*	reform	**re**-*form*
react	**re**-*act*		

Note: When a consonant or the letter **'a'** follows the prefix, a hyphen is not usually used, as in these two examples:

    rebound   rearrange

The *prefix 'self-'* is used to show that a person is acting of one's own accord, such as:

    I have always been **self**-*employed*.

    I believe that I am a **self**-*motivated* individual.

Words with a Suffix

A *hyphen* is used after *suffixes*. Examples are:

-all	-away	-back	-by
-down	-in	-off	-on
-out	-over	-up	and others.

Here are a few examples of the above *suffixes*:

be-**all** and end-**all**	give-**away**	out-**back**	kick-**of**
stand-**by**	shut-**down**	check-**in**	knock-**out**
make-**over**	clean-**up**	try-**on**	

❀ Apostrophe (') ❀

Omission of Letters in a Contraction

Use an *apostrophe* to replace letters omitted in a shortened form of a word or group of words called a *contraction*:

Table 46. Omitting of Letters in a Contraction (Sample List)

Word	Contr.	Word	Contr.	Word	Contr.
are not	aren't	cannot	can't	did not	didn't
do not	don't	had not	hadn't	has not	hasn't
have not	haven't	I am	I'm	I have	I've
is not	isn't	let us	let's	they are	they're
we have	we've	will not	won't	you are	you're
he had he would	he'd	he will he shall	he'll	I had I would	I'd
she had she would	she'd	they will they shall	they'll	what is what has	what's

The use of a *contraction* is related to whom the writing is directed. In formal writing, such as: *memos, casual letters, emails*, or *blogs*, etc., *contractions* are acceptable. With formal writing, such as: for *academic* or *business purposes*, etc., then tone becomes more important and the use of *contractions* less likely.

With Possessive Nouns

See the section on *possessive nouns*.

❀ Parentheses ( ) and Brackets [ ] ❀

Parentheses ( )

Use *parentheses* to interject relevant text within other text to further clarify, inform or qualify the preceding idea. Text within *parentheses* shows less importance, such as:

> He finally showed up (although we had other things to occupy our time), so we cheerfully continued with the presentation, without further delay.

Note:

1. Normal punctuation is used within *parentheses* if a full sentence is written (most of the time this will be a *comma*, *period*, or a *full-stop*).

2. *Dashes* should be used if emphasis is needed, such as:

> He finally showed up—even though we had been waiting for more than three hours, frustrated and annoyed—we continued reluctantly.

Use *parentheses* to inject an option within text:

> He finally showed up (bad traffic I reckon) so we continued with the presentation.

Use *parentheses* to note the year of a particular publication and any page number within that publication that a reference was taken. The full reference would need to be listed at the conclusion of the main text under the title 'References.' Here is an example:

Within Text (APA Formatting):

> *Martin Luther King Jr., (1958) was an American Baptist Minister, an activist and a prominent leader in the American civil rights movement. He said that, "Men often hate each other because they fear each other; they fear each other because they don't know each other; they don't know each other because they cannot communicate; they cannot communicate because they are separated." (p. 20)*

Reference (s):

> King Jr., M. L. (1958). *Stride toward freedom: The Montgomery story.* New York, NY: Harper.

Use *parentheses* within a sentence to enclose numbers or letters used for listed items, such as:

> We require a Marketing Manager to fill the position who can (1) protect our brand, (2) increase cash-flow by 15%, (3) have vision, and (4) blend into the company's culture seamlessly.

Use *partial* or *full parentheses* for lists using numbers and letters, as in:

a) salt	b) pepper	c) sugar	d) flour
(a) salt	(b) pepper	(c) sugar	(d) flour

Brackets [ ]

Use *brackets* as insertion marks to inject additional information, clarify [reduce uncertainty], reinforce, criticize or explain, a particular word or phrase, which would not normally be part of the sentence, such as:

> I observed John as he approached the panel. He wore a bright red [magenta] suit to the interview. It was a good thing that I was wearing my sunglasses!

Use *brackets* to inject the writer's opinion, which may or may not be in context, such as:

> John Lennon was murdered [or assassinated] on 8 December, 1980 (aged 40), in New York city, United States of America.

Use *brackets* when inserting comments or information that is not part of the original quote and / or may not be essential, such as:

> "And so, my fellow Americans: ask not what your country can do for you - ask what you can do for your country. My fellow citizens of the world: ask not what America will do for you, but what together we can do for the freedom of man [in a completely non-chauvinist form of the word *'man'*]."

Use *brackets* for editorial information, such as:

> To enclose parenthetical information that appears inside other parenthetical information. For example:
>
>> The director / producer (Peter Jackson, [born 31 October, 1961]), made famous by the trilogy 'Lord of the Rings,' also made many other hit movies.
>>
>> Peter Jackson (My friend of five years [the sale's clerk, not the celebrity movie producer from New Zealand], and the man I would trust with my life) is coming to dinner.

Use *brackets* around the *Latin adverb 'sic'* [sic] to indicate and highlight a recognized misspelled word or minor error in a quotation:

> "There were eigt [sic] workers who were found alive at the building site accident. Twenty-two were not so lucky."

QUOTE:

"It is not the answer that enlightens, but the question."

Eugene Ionesco

Double and Single Quotation Marks (" ") (' ')

Use *double quotation marks* to encapsulate a direct quote, such as:

She asked, "John, what time will you leave for the concert?"

However, a quotation is not needed with the following example:

She asked John what time he would leave for the concert.*

***Note:** the two example sentences above differ in meaning.

Use *single quotation marks* to encapsulate a quote within a *double quotation-marked direct quote*, such as:

John said, "Jim asked, 'What time will you leave for the concert?'"

Use *single quotation marks* to set off a nickname or to show shortened versions of names. Examples are:

Dimetrios Georgios Synodinos (1918 to 1996), also known as 'Jimmy the Greek' Snyder, was an American sports commentator.

'Christopher Neil' [Christopher Neil Linton] is a New Zealand born musician who released two pop-ballads in British Columbia, Canada (1982), with limited success. His single was also released in New Zealand, the rest of Canada, and The United States.

Almost always, place a *period* or *comma* inside a closing *double* and *single quotation mark*. Examples are:

The crosswalk lights changed from "Walk," to "Don't Walk," to "Walk" several times in a relatively short period-of-time.

John said, "I found my keys."

Capital Letters (Aa Bb Cc)

Use *capital letters*, also known as *'Upper Case'* letters in the following situations:

1. The first word of any sentence.
2. All proper nouns. Here are several examples:

   Title and / or name of a person: *Governor Lee, SGT. Kay, ...*
   Places: *The United Kingdom, Vancouver B.C., Canada, ...*
   Territories: *Virgin Islands, Victoria, Northern Territories, ...*
   Regions: *Kanagawa Prefecture in Japan, East Africa, ...*
   Provinces: *Nova Scotia, The Western Cape, Limerick, ...*

States: *Georgia, Idaho, New Jersey, ...*
Parishes: *Surrey, Essex, North Yorkshire, Lancashire, ...*
Districts: *Ashbourne District, District of Pi Pizzeria, ...*
Things: *Queen Mary II (Ship), Bismarck, Apollo 13, ...*
Days of the week: *Monday to Sunday.*
Months of the year: *January to December.*
Holidays: *Thanksgiving, Children's Day, Al Hijra, ...*
Festivals: *Lunar New Year Festival or Maudi Graw, ...*

3. A person's title when it precedes their name, but not capitalized when the title is acting as a description following the name, such as:

    Sergeant Jones is a hero.
    > *not*

    James Jones, a sergeant, is a hero.

4. An official company or organization's title and / or its abbreviation. Examples are:

    The New Zealand Qualification's Authority or NZQA

    The Federal Bureau of Investigation or FBI

    The Bureau, or FBI, was fast approaching its 50th anniversary.

5. The first and last words of a publication title, but not function words within a title, such as: *a, an, as, but, if, or, nor* and *the* or prepositions, regardless of their length. Examples are:

    The Power of the Platform: Speakers on Purpose.

    Chicken Soup for the Soul.

    Capitalize other words within a title, including the short verb forms *are, be,* and *is, etc.* Examples are:

    Men Are from Mars, Women Are from Venus.

    What Color Is Your Parachute?

6. Course names. Examples are:

    Reflecting on Professional Practice .... Algebra 101
    Leading in Diverse Cultures .... Intro. to Art

7. The first word of a salutation or complementary clause:

    Dear John   To whom it may concern
    Sincerely yours   With kindness

8. Cardinal points when they refer to specific regions, but not when they refer to directions, as in:

   I live on the North Island of New Zealand.

   or *'north'* un-capitalized, as in:

   I will travel up north today.

⌘ Inconspicuous Stressing: *Italics* ⌘

To *emphasize* a word or phrase and avoid the **'blackness effect'** on a page [not wanting text to jump out from other words in a conspicuous manner], styles are used such as *italics* or *oblique* scripts.

Italics are normally used for words and phrases in the following manner:

1. To *emphasize* words and phrases. Examples are:

   Kyoto, Japan boasts 17 properties listed as world heritage sites. The *old* temples and shrines on these properties, with their intricate gardens, are breathtakingly beautiful.

   Do not use a *CAPITALIZED WORD* or *WORDS* for emphasis; use ***bold italics*** instead.

2. The title of complete works. Examples are:

   Have you read the book called *The Power of the Platform*?

   Do you subscribe to *Time* magazine?

   Did you see the cover story in the *New York Times* newspaper?

   I am going to play *Fiddler on the Roof* this Sunday.

   Isn't *Gone with the Wind* a wonderful classic movie?

   I always watch the *20 / 20* investigative reporting show on the TV each week.

   Have you seen the *Mona Lisa* [also known as *La Gioconda* or *La Joconde*] painted by Leonardo di ser Piero da Vinci?

   John Lennon released the album *Imagine* in 1971.

3. Names of aircraft, ships, and trains. Examples are:

   The *Hughes Aircraft Company* was responsible for designing and building the Hughes H-4 Hercules, also known as the *Spruce Goose*.

The *Bismarck* was a famous German battleship during the Second World War.

The New Zealand Railways North Island cross-country train, called the *Blue Streak,* operated between 1968 and 1977.

4. Foreign words used in an English sentence, such as:

   After visiting the many children around Paris, I said goodbye to France, no, *Au revoir les enfants* [French for 'Goodbye, Children'].

5. Words and letters discussed as words and letters within a sentence, such as:

   The ***'-y'*** in a singular noun form is changed to ***'-ie'*** in most cases, such as: lady to ladies or baby to babies.

Bolding

Bold fonts are used to increase contrast with *emphasis* between main text and body text: Headings, subheadings and / or titles, or to highlight important sections or points. ***Bold fonts*** should be used sparingly!

Here is an example taken from a personal development book called, *How to Make People Like You in 90 Seconds*, by Nicholas Boothman (2000).

Heading: **5. Actions Do Speak Louder Than Words**

Subheading: **Body Language**

Section Title: ***Flirting***

Emphasized Text (indented and bold italics are used):

"Appearing sincere, or congruent, is a key ingredient for building the trust that opens the door to likeability and rapport.

Make sure that your words, your tonality and your gestures are all saying the same thing. Be on the lookout for incongruity in others. Notice how it makes you feel.

We've all seen those old movies where a couple of people are driving along in a car, and they're rocking the steering wheel even though the background..." (p. 60)

Bullet Points

Use *bullet points* to highlight important information in an unnumbered list, so that the reader can identify key points of fact quickly. Here are some basic points to consider when using *bullet points*:

1. The sentence introducing a *bulleted list* should always end with a colon (:).
2. If the text after the *bullet point* is a complete sentence, it must begin with a capital letter. Ending punctuation is good practice, but not essential, such as:
   - The first letter in a sentence must be capitalized.
   - All proper nouns must be capitalized.
3. If the text is not a full sentence, a *capital letter* is optional; styling is the main consideration when considering *capital letters* in this situation. Ending punctuation is not required. Here are examples:
   - the first letter in a sentence
   - proper nouns
4. Begin each *bullet point* or sentence using the same word class (or part of speech) such as the use of action verbs. Also keep the tense or future time usage consistent. For example:
   - **teach** five lessons a day for a week
   - **learn** three new concepts each month
   - **develop** two new lessons each quarter
5. *Bullet points* are used to summarize main points, should be visually appealing, and easy to read. For greater impact keep the sentences or text short and use bulleted lists sparingly.

QUOTE:

"Nostalgia is like a grammar lesson; you find the present tense and the past perfect."

Owens Lee Pomeroy

CHAPTER THREE: WRITING GUIDE

THE WRITING PROCESS

COMPOSITION and ACADEMIC WRITING

Many composition and academic writing classes emphasize that writing is an organized process. One such process is to divide the work into five main stages, with these main stages often subdivided into more discrete steps or parts. The main stages are:

1. Prewriting,
2. Drafting,
3. Revising and Editing,
4. Proofing, and
5. Submitting or Publishing.

✿ Prewriting: Organizing Thoughts ✿

Elements of *pre-writing* may include planning, researching, outlining, diagraming, storyboarding or clustering. Prior to writing, an opportunity to ask directed questions could be given:

1. What is the purpose for creating the composition / manuscript?
2. Who is the target audience, and will the topic be of high interest, or value to them?
3. What is the specific *'point of difference'* that makes the story, information, or message more captivating or of higher value than other writers of similar material?

Try to get a writer to compose for a purpose other than to please the teacher, solely focused on achieving a good grade, or to satisfy a course requirement. If the writer writes with purpose, they are more likely to become self-motivated rather than pressure driven.

Choose a topic relevant to the writer's real life. In fact, have them directed toward the goal of reading the composition to a person or group of their choosing at completion. When the appropriate support is given, this simple dynamic will create motivation, purpose and a higher quality of work.

Get the writer to conduct real research on their topic. Task them to gather five to ten facts to support their idea, either by using the school or local library, or the internet. Get the writer to document the source of the information that they have gathered, such as: URL links to music videos, photos, or web sites. They should also reference the author, date of publication for books and magazines, or any other sources used [A.P.A. or Harvard Formatting]. It is also very important to educate the writer about plagiarism and copyright infringement.

Once the writer has researched and gathered information, a circle discussion can be held where all writers can 'show-and-tell' their topic to the group. This generates teacher-peer feedback, useful information to assist the writer as they organize their topic toward the next step, a mind map.

Mind Mapping

A *mind or bubble map*—also called a *spider diagram*, or an *idea clustering*—is a graphical method of planning ideas, to present a vision in an organized sequential way. These organizational maps generally take on a hierarchical, tree branch, or spider-legs format of connected ideas, with these ideas branching off into subsections. A mind map can be used for a single paragraph or to create a composition or essay.

There are two main reasons to create and use a *mind map*. They are:

1. to organize initial thoughts, and
2. to serve as a cue, to trigger memory while writing.
3. The mind map used for my previous book called *English Language Grammar Reference & Teacher's Guide* (C. Neil Linton, 2012) was a spider-diagram (see Diagram 1.) and is shown here as an example; however, it is important to understand that the mapping process used may differ from one individual to another, so adapting an individual style that works best may be necessary:

Step one: The main idea; working title or concept (the body).

A small rounded rectangle was drawn in the center of the page, representing the main theme or concept for the spider diagram (the body). The center rectangle was vertically split in half. In the right-half segment the words *Grammar Reference* was written. In the left-half segment the words *Teacher's Guide* was written.

Step two: Breaking the main themes down into manageable main ideas. In the book's example, this was the chapters. Seven primary spider-legs representing each chapter and the appendix [initially labeled '...Resources'], were drawn from the center rectangle; labeled with the working chapter's titles:

    Chapter One: English Words.
    Chapter Two: Punctuation, and so on.

Step three: Secondary Spider-legs.

Secondary spider-legs (curved lines) were then drawn from each primary spider-leg. These secondary spider-legs represent each of the chapter's sub-sections. In the case of *Chapter One: English Words*, the sub-section titles were:

    1. Nouns   2. Adjectives
    3. Pronouns   4. Verbs
    5. Adverbs   6. Prepositions
    7. Conjunctions   8. Interjections

Step four: Breaking it down into deeper subsections (the toes).

The sections were broken down into sub-sections, such as:

Conjunctions were broken down into three categories:
    1. Coordinating,
    2. Subordinating, and
    3. Correlative or Double.

Diagram 1. Spider Diagram used for this Book

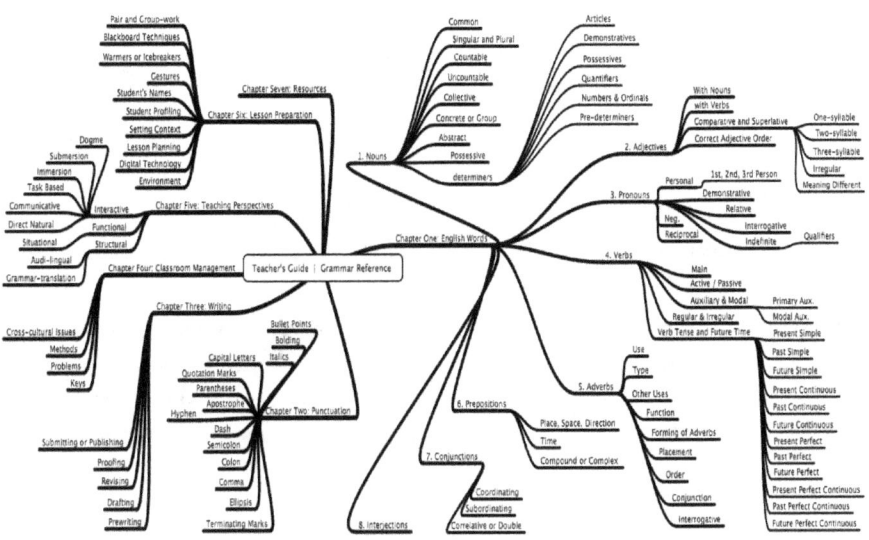

Diagram 2. Bubble Map

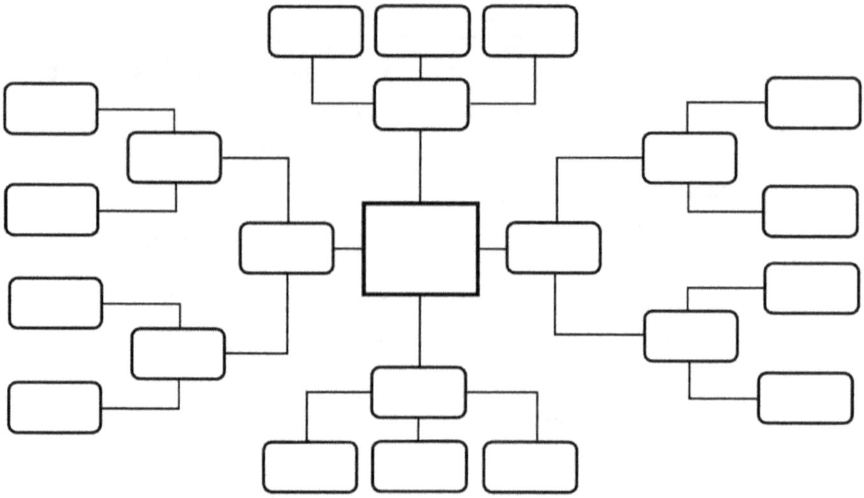

Drafting

After the pre-writing process has been achieved, the next process is to write a first draft. This process involves developing an overall holistic text, focused *'on topic'*, toward a specific word or page length.

Elements of a first draft may include:

1. identifying the central idea, argument, or theme,
2. converting mind map ideas into cohesively organized paragraphs that reflect the central idea, argument, or theme,
3. organizing supporting or opposing scientific or intellectual research, surveys, or other data, in the appropriate places, throughout the composition,
4. creating an effect flow from one idea to the next, by using transitional sentences.

The following section can be used for instruction on how to create a single paragraph, as an assignment, or to create multiple paragraphs for a larger writing project, such as a composition or essay, using transitional sentences to do so (see *Transitional Sentence*).

Paragraph Construction

The purpose of forming text into paragraphs is to express multiple points in an organized way. Each paragraph should express a single point, an idea, or an opinion that maintains sentence unity and coherence.

Each new paragraph should introduce a new topic, or be used to change speakers when writing dialog. Toward the conclusion of the presentation a paragraph or paragraphs provide a summary of the combined topics with a conclusion, or ending.

Although there are no specific rules on paragraph length, it is advised that paragraphs should not be so long that the drawn-out writing or dialog is likely to tire or overwhelm the reader. It is accepted practice to break a lengthy paragraph of one topic into related multiple topic specific paragraphs, to provide reading ease.

A paragraph is organized and expressed with three unified elements. These elements are:

1. A Topic Sentence,
2. Supporting Sentence (s), and
3. Concluding Sentence (s).

Topic Sentence

A *topic sentence* is a single sentence that introduces or states the topic for that paragraph, or if needed to introduce multiple paragraphs specific to that topic. This single sentence reflects the main idea, point, or opinion to be developed or explained. This sentence should contain a strong verb, assisting in creating a statement that stands out from other sentences in the paragraph or related paragraphs that follow.

>This is an example of a topic sentence:
>
>>*Special needs students require additional support if they are to succeed academically and emotionally.*

Each subsequent sentence in the same paragraph, or multiple paragraphs specific to that topic should be relevant; providing unity throughout the paragraph or multiple paragraphs.

Supporting Sentences

Supporting sentences are one or more sentences that strengthen the preceding *topic sentence*. Supporting sentences often provide the evidence to support the topic, such as: facts, statistics, examples, logical reasoning, quotes or a reference or references of other intellectual contributors on the topic.

This is an example of a supporting sentence:

> *In fact, studies have shown that special needs students who are correctly identified and supported consistently achieve higher academic scores on tests. Clinical analysis further suggests that this support greatly improves self-confidence and self-worth, providing students with the increased ability to focus more intensely on academic materials.*

Concluding Sentences

Concluding sentences are one or more sentences that consolidate the paragraph's or paragraphs' supporting sentences before transitioning to the next topic and subsequent paragraphs.

This is an example of a concluding sentence:

> *Appropriate academic and emotional support are clearly required for special needs students to allow the best possible chances of success in their pursuit of studies and a happier life.*

Sentence Unity and Coherence

Sentence unity and coherence can be achieved by using transition words or phrases. Transition words and phrases can be used for many situations. Here are several examples:

For opening an initial paragraph, or for general use:

generally speaking	unquestionably	admittedly
nobody denies	assuredly	certainly
granted (that)	no doubt	obviously
of course	to be sure	undoubtedly
in general	at this level	in this situation

For continuing a common line of reasoning:

consequently	clearly, then	and furthermore
moreover	besides that	additionally
in addition	because	in the same way
following this	further	also
it is easy to see that	pursuing this further	in light of

To change the line of reasoning:

on the other hand	on the contrary	in contrast
nevertheless	but, *or* yet	however
in spite of	despite	even though

For comparison:

similarly	comparable	likewise
in the same way	just as	so too

For contrast:

however	notwithstanding	despite
on the other hand	rather	even so
on the contrary	in contrast	nonetheless
at the same time	though this may be	nevertheless
instead	alternatively	otherwise
still	but	and yet

For summary or for emphasis:

in short	in brief	in fact
in truth	in reality	in any event
in other words	in summary	indeed
in general	of course	remarkably
assuredly	definitely	certainly
as I stated	clearly	importantly
without doubt	generally	after all
I hope	naturally	it seems
on the whole		

For the final points of a paragraph or essay:

finally	lastly	in closing

To chronologically adjoin multiple paragraphs which link to the same topic sentence:

first, ...	second, ...	third, ...
generally	furthermore	finally
as well	also	lastly
in the first place	pursuing this further	basically
to be sure	additionally	similarly
just in the same way		

To signal a conclusion:

therefore	this concludes	hence
in final analysis	in conclusion	indeed
in the end	in final consideration	

To restate a point within a paragraph in another way or in a more exacting way:

| in other words | to reinforce this idea | specifically |
| that is to say | or | |

Sequence or time:

subsequently	afterwards	later
as soon as	after	before
at first	at last	at length
at that time	presently	recently
long	finally	as of late
in the first place	meanwhile	immediately
first, ...	second, ...	third, ...
in the future	in the meantime	in the past
soon	then	thereafter
eventually	currently	now
earlier	next	

✿ Misused Words ✿

Homonym, Homograph, Homophone

A *homonym* is two or more words having different meanings, but the same spelling and pronunciation, such as: race (n.) [a competition between runners] and race (n.) [a group of people sharing distinct physical characteristics or culture, history and language].

A *homograph* is two or more words having different meanings, the same spelling, but not necessarily pronounced the same, such as: bow (v.) [bend the head or upper part of the body as a sign of respect, greeting, or shame] and bow (n.) [bent or curved in shape].

A *homophone* is two or more words having different meanings and spelling, but the same pronunciation, such as: knew (v.) [past tense of the word 'know' - to understand a person, place or thing, etc.], and new (adj.) [not existing before, freshly or recently produced, introduced or discovered, etc.].

Table 47. Homonym, Homograph, and Homophone Definitions

Term	Meaning	Spelling	Pronunciation
Homonym	different	the same	the same
Homograph	different	the same	different
Homophone	different	different	the same

Common mistakes in English usage are often made not only by those that are learning the English language (speakers of other languages), but also by native speakers.

The most important thing to remember about any language is that the underlining purpose for language is to communicate a message. If a message is being passed on from one person to another, through spoken communication with a few common mistakes, then these common mistakes should be tolerated or acceptable [in the short-term], knowing that over time they can be corrected by the user, as language learning skills are developed. A sixty-percent correct usage tolerance in accepting a forty-percent error rate in a progressing new learner is acceptable.

Here are some examples of the most common misused words when writing and / or in speech [incorrect usage of accent, stress or pitch]:

    Accept (v.): to receive willingly, to approve, to agree
    Except (v., prep.): to exclude or to leave out

    Ad (n.): an advertisement
    Add (v.): to join, unite, combine or a mathematical sum

    Affect (v.): to cause a change in something or someone
    Effect (n.): a result

    Ate (v.): past tense of eat
    Eight (cardinal number): the number 8

    Bass (n.): a voice, instrument, or sound of low pitch [bass drum]
    Bass (n.): common European freshwater perch (fish)

    Buy (v.): to purchase
    By (prep., adv.): next to, beside, by way of something
    Bye (n.): to express farewell (abbreviation for the word 'goodbye')

    Cite (v.): to quote somebody as an example or as evidence
    Sight (v., n.): to aim through a scope, the ability to see or be seen
    Site (n.): the location of land or stored data (computer hard drive)

    Desert (v.): to abandon
    Dessert (n.): a sweet food

Dove (v.): past tense of dive
Dove (n.): a pigeon-like bird with a cooing voice [a white dove]

Elicit (v.): to draw out a response
Illicit (adj.): forbidden by law, rules or custom

For (prep.): in support, benefit, or in favor of
Fore (n., adj.): the front part, situated, placed or located in the front
Four (cardinal number): the number 4

Knew (v.): past tense of know
New (adj.): not existing before, recently produced or discovered

Know (v.): to be familiar with someone or something
No (n., det.): not any, negative reply of refusal

Object (v.): to express one's disapproval or disagreement
Object (n.): a thing that can be seen, touched or felt

Peace (n.): freedom from disturbance, war or violence; tranquil
Piece (n.): portion of an object or material by separating the whole

Principal (n., adj.): a person with the highest authority or position, first in order of importance
Principle (n.): a fundamental truth or belief

Raw (adj.): uncooked
Roar (v., n.): a loud deep sound, a loud deep sound made by an animal [especially a Lion]

Subject (v.): to cause or force to undergo a particular experience
Subject (n.): a person or thing being discussed or described

Their (det.): belonging to people or things previously mentioned
There (adv.): a place or position
They're (contraction): the contracted form for 'they are'

To (prep.): to express motion, or express attachment
Too (adv.): to a higher degree than is wanted or permissible; usually placed at the end of a clause and means also   [e.g. I like it too].
Two (cardinal number): the number 2

Wander (v., n.): to walk around aimlessly, an act of wandering
Wonder (v., n.): a desire to know, a feeling of surprise

Weather (n.): atmospheric conditions
Whether (conj.): to express an opinion between two or more alternative possibilities

Ware (n.): a type of product as in 'stoneware or Wedgwood-ware'
Wear (v.): to have on one's body to clothe, decorate or protect
Where (adv.): in or to what place or location

Write (v.): to mark letters, words, or symbols on a surface
Right (adj.): morally good, justified, or acceptable

You're (contraction): the contracted form for 'you are'
Your (det.): belonging to that which the speaker is addressing

Composition, Essay, or Article

A *composition* is a collective body of sentences that has been organized into one or more paragraphs.

An *essay or article* is a short piece of nonfiction writing, which is usually written from an author's personal perspective. Essays are written for a number of purposes. A writer may want to:

1. analyze
2. propose
3. conclude
4. challenge
5. call readers to action
6. provide literary criticism
7. change attitudes
8. provoke thought
9. entertain
10. theorize
11. evaluate
12. recommend
13. express an observation
14. reflect
15. express feelings
16. request
17. give aesthetic pleasure
18. summarize
19. inform
20. persuade
21. publicly declare a political policy
22. provide instructions necessary to complete a task
23. argue for a particular point of view

Writers can be assigned to compose a short one paragraph composition, or with the use of transitional sentences can be coached toward writing more lengthy compositions, or a full essay of several hundred or thousand words, depending on their English language ability.

Transitional Sentence

A *transitional sentence* prepares and creates a smooth passage or evolution from one paragraph to the next. A successfully written transitional sentence will allow the reader to logically connect the topic and its supporting content of the previously read paragraph with the topic and supporting content of the upcoming paragraph.

This is an example of a transitional sentence that leads to the next topic:

> Clearly, appropriate academic and emotional support are two key ingredients to improving the best possible chance for success in special needs students, as they pursue their studies and seek a happier life. **However, proactive positive parent involvement is also essential and necessary.**

✣ Revising and Editing ✣

Drafting, revising and *editing* are the processes where a writer develops an overall holistic text, which is refined toward a finished work or final draft, to a specific word or page length. The processes of drafting and revising often overlap, as the writing process moves back and forth between the two stages.

Revision is an important stage in the writing process where the writer reviews the entire draft, and as needed, organizes, condenses, corrects sentences, paragraphs or sections and then adds additional information attempting to produce an accurate, consistent, and complete work. The writing process may involve many drafts requiring multiple revisions.

The editing process often begins with the author's preceding stages of drafting, revising and editing, continuing with collaboration between the author and / or authors and the editor and / or editors.

Editing involves reviewing text and identifying usage errors and ensuring style adherence. It also includes the correction of grammatical errors and inconsistencies in usages, misspellings, typographical errors (typos), the correction of punctuation and correcting errors in citations.

It is critical that a chosen editor is familiar with the subject being edited, or at least possess a passion for gaining additional personal knowledge for the topic. An editor must have refined essential skills, able to:

1. work to deadlines,
2. be reliable,
3. be accessible,
4. be ethical,
5. respect confidentiality,
6. pay attention to detail,
7. sustain prolonged focus while on task,
8. have good interpersonal skills; tact, and
9. most importantly, be compatible with the writer or writers.

✂ Proofing ✂

Proofreading is the final step before submitting work to an assessor, literary agent or publisher. The act of proofreading should be performed by the original writer, on the first and final occasion; however, writers usually have low energy levels and mental fatigue toward the end of the writing process, are often burdened with stress, and usually blind to their own errors. The inclusion of a qualified third-party (s) to proofread prior to the final review is essential (not the editor or editors of the project). This additional *'set-of-eyes'* should result in a higher quality of work.

✂ Submitting or Publishing ✂

Submitting

When *submitting* a composition of any kind, whether it be an assignment, report, journal or magazine article, or an essay, a writer should follow the strict guidelines outlined by the receiving organization. It is advised that a writer familiarize themselves with any relevant guidelines before the first word is written or typed.

Publishing

The question that a writer may be pondering is whether to self-publish or to submit their work directly to a literary agent or a publisher. Manuscripts that are submitted directly to a publisher are referred to as *unsolicited submissions*. These submissions are usually placed in a general pile, where the publisher's readers browse through them to identify the most appealing commercial manuscripts of sufficient quality with the greatest revenue potential, to be eventually referred to an acquisitions editor (s) for review.

Once the acquisitions editor (s) have narrowed down their choices from thousands of submissions, they send the manuscript to editorial staff. It's important to realize that unsolicited submissions have a very low rate of being accepted, with a very small percentage published; said to be about 2-5 percent of all annual manuscripts submitted to the publishing industry in the United States.

The alternative is to find a literary agent, or to self-publish If self-publishing is of interest, a writer or author has access to a number of new technological publishing tools, resources, and services that are available from the self-publishing industry. Writers can self-publish their work as an e-book, where a manuscript is uploaded to a website from where it can be downloaded and read by anyone, or they can utilize the user-friendly cost-effective *'print-on-demand'* option.

Here are several print-on-demand online companies. This list has been provided with the intension of assisting with a starting point toward research and investigation.

Disclaimer: Use the following list at your own risk and / or discretion:

AA Printing	http://www.printshopcentral.com
Advantage Medina Group	http://www.amgbook.com
Angel Printing San Diego	http://www.angelprint.com
Apex Book Manufacturing	http://www.apexbm.com
Art Book Bindery	http://www.artbookbindery.com
Authorhouse	http://www.authorhouse.com
Aventine Press	http://www.aventinepress.com
Blitz Print Inc.	http://www.blitzprint.com
Blurb	http://www.blurb.com
Book Stand Publishing	http://www.ebookstand.com
Booklocker	http://www.booklocker.com
Createspace*	**http://www.createspace.com**
Dog Ear	http://www.eigology.com/dogear
Equilibrium	http://www.equilibriumbooks.com
Foremost Press	http://foremostpress.com
Infinity Publishing*	http://www.infinitypublishing.com
Inkwater Press	http://www.inkwaterpress.com
Instant (Fundcraft) Publishing	http://www.instantpublisher.com
iUniverse	http://www.iuniverse.com
Llumina	http://www.llumina.com
Lulu*	**http://www.lulu.com**
Outskirts Press	http://www.outskirtspress.com
Pleasant Word (WinePress)	http://www.pleasantword.com
Trafford	http://www.trafford.com
Virtual Bookworm	http://www.virtualbookworm.com
WingSpan*	http://www.wingspanpress.com
Wordclay*	http://www.wordclay.com
Xlibris*	http://www2.xlibris.com
Xulon Press	http://www.xulonpress.com

* Sites that I found inviting.

APPENDIX

STUDENT RESOURCES

✼ Dialogs and Role-plays ✼

Table 50. Dialog Practice Suggestions for Various Contexts

Context	Purpose	Suggested Language
Introductions	Expressing personal information Finding out more information about other people	A: What's your name? B: My name is <u>Mr. Chris, your English teacher</u>. A: Where are you from? B: I'm from <u>the United States</u>. ***Expanded Dialog:*** A: Where do you live? B: I live in <u>Yokohama City</u>, near <u>Tokyo</u>.
Daily Routine	Asking about another person's activities	A: What time do you <u>start school</u>? B: I <u>start school</u> at <u>08:30</u>. A: What time do you eat <u>lunch</u>? B: I eat <u>lunch</u> from <u>12:30</u> to <u>13:00</u>. ***Expanded Dialog:*** A: What do you eat for <u>lunch</u>? B: I like to eat <u>sandwiches</u> for <u>lunch</u>.

Context	Purpose	Suggested Language
In the Neighborhood	Asking and receiving directions Asking distance	A: Where can I find the bank? B: The bank is next to McDonalds. A: Where is the bakery? B: The bakery is across from the bar. ***Expanded Dialog:*** A: How far is the library? B: Only about ten minutes on foot.
Job Interview	Introducing yourself Responding to questions directed at you	A: Good morning. What's your name? B: My name is Christopher from Yokohama. A: What position would you like? B: I'm interested in administration. ***Expanded Dialog:*** A: Do you have any experience? B: Yes, I do. I worked for the University of Tokyo for 15 years.
At the Mall	Getting instructions	A: Where can I buy a digital HD TV? B: You can buy a digital HD TV at the home-center. A: Where is the home-center? B: The home-center is next to McDonalds restaurant. ***Expanded Dialog:*** A: Is the home-center open on the weekend? B: Yes! The home-center is open from 08:00 to 18:00.

Context	Purpose	Suggested Language
At the Train Station At the Travel Agent	Getting and giving information Asking the price Buying a ticket Information clarification	A: What time does <u>the express train</u> depart from <u>New York</u> to <u>Chicago</u>? B: <u>The express train</u> for <u>Chicago</u> departs <u>daily</u> at <u>08:00</u>. A: How much is a one-way ticket? B: A one-way ticket costs <u>$78.00</u>. A: How much is a round-trip ticket? B: A round-trip ticket costs <u>$139.00</u>. ***Expanded Dialog:*** A: I'll have a round-trip ticket departing on <u>November 21</u> and returning on <u>December 25</u>, please. A: Where does the train leave from? B: The express train for <u>Chicago</u> leaving on <u>November 21</u>, at <u>08:00</u> departs from <u>platform 2</u>.
The Weather	Getting weather information	A: What do you think the weather will be like <u>tomorrow</u>? B: It will be <u>cloudy</u>. A: What do you think the weather will be like <u>this weekend</u>? B: It will be <u>sunny and warm</u>. ***Expanded Dialog:*** A: Should I bring <u>a coat</u>, just in case? B: Yes! <u>You should wear layered clothing in this environment</u>.

Context	Purpose	Suggested Language
At a Restaurant	Talking about food Ordering	A: What are you going to order? B: I'll have <u>a hamburger-steak</u>. A: I'm going to have <u>the fried rice</u>. A: What would you like to drink? B: I'll have <u>a diet coke</u>. A: I'll just have <u>some ice-water</u>. ***Expanded Dialog:*** C: May I take your order? B: Yes, please! I'll have <u>a hamburger-steak</u> and my friend will have <u>the fried rice</u>. C: Would you like anything to drink? A: Yes, please! My friend will have <u>a diet coke</u> and we'll both have some <u>ice-water</u>. Thank you!
Living Environment	Making choices Describing activities	A: Where would you like to live? B: I'd like to live in the <u>country</u>! A: Why do you like the <u>country</u>? B: Because I like <u>nature</u>, <u>open spaces</u> and <u>fresh air</u>. ***Expanded Dialog:*** A: What can you do in the <u>country</u>? B: You can <u>go fishing</u> or <u>hike in the mountains</u>.
School Life	Expressing your interests	A: How's your school life going? B: It's OK, but I'm thinking <u>about joining a sport's club</u>. A: What are you interested in? B: I like <u>tennis</u>!

List of Irregular Verbs

Table 51. Irregular Verbs

Base Form	Past Simple	Past Participle	3rd Person Singular	Present Participle / Gerund (–ing form)
abide	abode abided	abode abided abidden	abides	abiding
alight	alit / alighted	alit / alighted	alights	alighting
arise	arose	arisen	arises	arising
awake	awoke	awoken	awakes	awaking
be	was / were	been	is	being
bear	bore	born / borne	bears	bearing
beat	beat	Beaten / beat	beats	beating
become	became	become	becomes	becoming
begin	began	begun	begins	beginning
behold	beheld	beheld	beholds	beholding
bend	bent	bent	bends	bending
bet	betted / bet	betted / bet	bets	betting
bid	bade / bid	bidden / bid	bids	bidding
bid	bid	bid	bids	bidding
bind	bound	bound	binds	binding
bite	bit	bitten / bit	bites	biting
bleed	bled	bled	bleeds	bleeding
blow	blew	blow / blowed	blows	blowing
break	broke	broken	breaks	breaking
breed	bred	bred	breeds	breeding
bring	brought	brought	brings	bringing
broadcast	broadcast broadcasted	broadcast broadcasted	broadcasts	broadcasting

build	built	built	builds	building
burn	burnt / burned	burnt / burned	burns	burning
burst	burst	burst	bursts	bursting
bust	bust / busted	bust / busted	busts	busting
buy	bought	bought	buys	buying
cast	cast	cast	casts	casting
catch	caught	caught	catches	catching
choose	chose	chosen	chooses	choosing
clap	clapped / clapt	clapped / clapt	claps	clapping
cling	clung	clung	clings	clinging
clothe	clad / clothed	clad / clothed	clothes	clothing
come	came	come	comes	coming
cost	cost / costed	cost / costed	costs	costing
creep	crept	crept	creeps	creeping
cut	cut	cut	cuts	cutting
dare	dared / durst	dared	dares	daring
deal	dealt	dealt	deals	dealing
dig	dug	dug	digs	digging
dive	dived / dove	dived	dives	diving
do	did	done	does	doing
draw	drew	drawn	draws	drawing
dream	dreamt / dreamed	dreamt / dreamed	dreams	dreaming
drink	drank	drank / drunk	drinks	drinking
drive	drove	driven	drives	driving
dwell	dwelt / dwelled	dwelt / dwelled	dwells	dwelling
eat	ate	eaten	eats	eating
fall	fell	fallen	falls	falling
feed	fed	fed	feeds	feeding

feel	felt	felt	feels	feeling
fight	fought	fought	fights	fighting
find	found	found	finds	finding
fit	fit/fitted	fit/fitted	fits	fitting
flee	fled	fled	flees	fleeing
fling	flung	flung	flings	flinging
fly	flew / flied	flown / flied	flies	flying
forbid	forbade forbad	forbidden forbad	forbids	forbidding
forecast	forecast forecasted	forecast forecasted	forecasts	forecasting
foresee	foresaw	foreseen	foresees	foreseeing
foretell	foretold	foretold	foretells	foretelling
forget	forgot	forgotten	forgets	forgetting
forgive	forgave	forgiven	forgives	forgiving
forsake	forsook	forsaken	forsakes	forsaking
freeze	froze	frozen	freezes	freezing
frostbite	frostbit	frostbitten	frostbites	frostbiting
get	got	got/gotten	gets	getting
give	gave	given	gives	giving
go	went	gone	goes	going
grind	ground	ground	grinds	grinding
grow	grew	grown	grows	growing
handwrite	handwrote	handwritten	handwrites	handwriting
hang	hung hanged	hung hanged	hangs	hanging
have	had	had	has	having
hear	heard	heard	hears	hearing
hide	hid	hidden / hid	hides	hiding
hit	hit	hit	hits	hitting
hold	held	held	holds	holding

hurt	hurt	hurt	hurts	hurting
inlay	inlaid	inlaid	inlays	inlaying
input	input inputted	input inputted	inputs	inputting
interlay	interlaid	interlaid	interlays	interlaying
keep	kept	kept	keeps	keeping
kneel	knelt kneeled	knelt kneeled	kneels	kneeling
knit	knit / knitted	knit / knitted	knits	knitting
know	knew	known	knows	knowing
lay	laid	laid	lays	laying
lead	led	led	leads	leading
lean	leant leaned	leant leaned	leans	leaning
leap	leapt leaped	leapt leaped	leaps	leaping
learn	learnt learned	learnt learned	learns	learning
leave	left	left	leaves	leaving
lend	lent	lent	lends	lending
let	let	let	lets	letting
lie	lay	lain	lies	lying
light	lit / lighted	lit / lighted	lights	lighting
lose	lost	lost	loses	losing
make	made	made	makes	making
mean	meant	meant	means	meaning
meet	met	met	meets	meeting
melt	melted	molten melted	melts	melting
mislead	misled	misled	misleads	misleading
mistake	mistook	mistaken	mistakes	mistaking
mis-understand	mis-understood	mis-understood	mis-understands	mis-understanding

mow	mowed	mown / mowed	mows	mowing
overdraw	overdrew	overdrawn	overdraws	overdrawing
overhear	overheard	overheard	overhears	overhearing
overtake	overtook	overtaken	overtakes	overtaking
pay	paid	paid	pays	paying
preset	preset	preset	presets	presetting
prove	proved	proven / proved	proves	proving
put	put	put	puts	putting
quit	quit / quitted	quit / quitted	quits	quitting
read	read	read	reads	reading
rid	rid / ridded	rid / ridded	rids	ridding
ride	rode / rid	ridden	rides	riding
ring	rang	rung	rings	ringing
rise	rose	risen	rises	rising
rive	rived	riven / rived	rives	riving
run	ran	run	runs	running
saw	sawed	sawn / sawed	saws	sawing
say	said	said	says	saying
see	saw	seen	sees	seeing
seek	sought	sought	seeks	seeking
sell	sold	sold	sells	selling
send	sent	sent	sends	sending
set	set	set	sets	setting
sew	sewed	sewn / sewed	sews	sewing
shake	shook	shaken	shakes	shaking
shave	shaved	shaven / shaved	shaves	shaving
shear	shore / sheared	shorn / sheared	shears	shearing
shed	shed	shed	sheds	shedding

shine	shone shinned	shone shinned	shines	shining
shoe	shod	shod	shoes	shoeing
shoot	shot	shot	shoots	shooting
show	showed	shown showed	shows	showing
shrink	shrank shrunk	shrunk shrunken	shrinks	shrinking
shut	shut	shut	shuts	shutting
sing	sang	sung	sings	singing
sink	sank sunk	sunk sunken	sinks	sinking
sit	sat	sat	sits	sitting
slay	slew / slayed	slain / slayed	slays	slaying
sleep	slept	slept	sleeps	sleeping
slide	slid	slid slidden	slides	sliding
sling	slung	slung	slings	slinging
slink	slunk	slunk	slinks	slinking
slit	slit	slit	slits	slitting
smell	smelt smelled	smelt smelled	smells	smelling
sneak	sneaked snuck	sneaked snuck	sneaks	sneaking
sow	sowed	sown sowed	sows	sowing
speak	spoke spake	spoken	speaks	speaking
speed	sped speeded	sped speeded	speeds	speeding
spell	spelt spelled	spelt spelled	spells	spelling
spend	spent	spent	spends	spending
spill	spilt spilled	spilt spilled	spills	spilling

spin	span / spun	spun	spins	spinning
spit	spat / spit	spat / spit	spits	spitting
split	split	split	splits	splitting
spoil	spoilt / spoiled	spoilt / spoiled	spoils	spoiling
spread	spread	spread	spreads	spreading
spring	sprang / sprung	sprung	springs	springing
stand	stood	stood	stands	standing
steal	stole	stolen	steals	stealing
stick	stuck	stuck	sticks	sticking
sting	stung	stung	stings	stinging
stink	stank / stunk	stunk	stinks	stinking
stride	strode	stridden	strides	striding
strike	struck	struck / stricken	strikes	striking
string	strung	strung	strings	stringing
strip	stript / stripped	stript / stripped	strips	stripping
strive	strove / strived	striven / strived	strives	striving
sublet	sublet	sublet	sublets	subletting
sunburn	sunburned / sunburnt	sunburned / sunburnt	sunburns	sunburning
swear	swore	sworn	swears	swearing
sweat	sweat / sweated	sweat / sweated	sweats	sweating
sweep	swept / sweeped	swept / sweeped	sweeps	sweeping
swell	swelled	swollen / swelled	swells	swelling
swim	swam	swum	swims	swimming
swing	swung	swung	swings	swinging

take	took	taken	takes	taking
teach	taught	taught	teaches	teaching
tear	tore	torn	tears	tearing
tell	told	told	tells	telling
think	thought	thought	thinks	thinking
thrive	throve thrived	thriven thrived	thrives	thriving
throw	threw	thrown	throws	throwing
thrust	thrust	thrust	thrusts	thrusting
tread	trod	trod / trodden	treads	treading
undergo	underwent	undergone	undergoes	undergoing
understand	understood	understood	understands	understanding
undertake	undertook	undertaken	undertakes	undertaking
upset	upset	upset	upsets	upsetting
wake	woke waked	woken waked / woke	wakes	waking
wear	wore	worn	wears	wearing
weave	wove weaved	woven weaved	weaves	weaving
wed	wed wedded	wed wedded	weds	wedding
weep	wept	wept	weeps	weeping
wet	wet wetted	wet wetted	wets	wetting
win	won	won	wins	winning
wind	wound winded	wound winded	winds	winding
withdraw	withdrew	withdrawn	withdraws	withdrawing
withhold	withheld	withheld	withholds	withholding
withstand	withstood	withstood	withstands	withstanding
wring	wrung	wrung	wrings	wringing
write	wrote / writ	written / writ	writes	writing

 Abbreviations Common in English Words

Table 52. Abbreviations Common in English

A

a.	adjective (in early volumes)	adj.	adjective
adv.	adverb	adv. phr.	adverb phrase
Amer.	American	Amer. Eng.	American English
app.	Appendix	applic.	application
Aug.	August	AU	Australia
AT	Austria	aux. v.	auxiliary verb

C

CA	Canada	c.	century
c.	Chapter (reference)	coll.	college
concr.	concrete	conj.	conjunction
const.	constructed with	corresp.	correspondence

D

Dan.	Danish	Dec.	December
def. art.	definite article	demonstr.	demonstrative
demonstr. adj.	demonstrative adjective	demonstr. pron.	demonstrative pronoun
det.	determiner	DK	Denmark
dial.	dialect	Du.	Dutch

E

early ME	early Middle English	Eccl. L.	Ecclesiastical Latin
Eccl.	Ecclesiastes	eccl.	ecclesiastic (al)
Ed.	edition, editor	Ed. *or* ed.	Education
EG	Egypt	ellipt.	elliptical
Eng.	England; English	equiv. to	equivalent to
esp.	especially	etc.	et cetera

133

F

FJ	Fiji	FI	Finland
FR	France	F.	French
Feb.	February	fem.	feminine / female
f.n.	footnote	F. / Fri.	Friday

G

Gael.	Gaelic (Scots)	gen.	General (-ly)
Germ.	German	DE	Germany
GK / Gk	Greek	Glos.	Glossary
GR	Greece	GL	Greenland

I

imper. imp. impv.	imperative	indef.	indefinite
indef. art.	indefinite article	inf. / infin.	infinitive
infl.	inflected, inflection	int. / interj.	interjection
Inter'l Int.	International	interrog. pron.	interrogative pronoun
intr.	intransitive	intrans.	intransitive
intro. introd.	introduction introduce	IE	Ireland
Ir.	Irish / Ireland	irreg.	irregular
IL	Israel	It.	Italian / Italy
IT	Italy	IT	Information Technology

J

Jan.	January	JP	Japan

L

L.	Latin	late L.	late Latin
LG	Low German	l. L.	Late Latin
L. / Lon.	London	lit.	Literal (-ly) / literature

M

MY	Malaysia	marg.	margin
masc.	masculine	M. / Mon.	Monday

N

NP	Napal	NL	Netherlands
n.	noun / note / name / new / national		
n. phr.	noun phrase	n. pl.	noun plural
Nat.	National	N. Isl.	North Island
north.	northern	Nov.	November
No. num.	Numeral (-s)	N.Z. (NZ)	New Zealand Aotearoa
NO	Norway	–	–

O

obs.	obsolete	occas.	occasionally
Oct.	October	OE	Old English
OED	Oxford English Dictionary	orig.	original

P

p.	paragraph / part / participle / person / past / population		
p. / pp.	page	pers. pron.	personal pronoun
Pg.	Portuguese	phr.	phrase(s)
pl.	place	plur.	plural
possess.	possessive	Pos.	positive
p.p.	past participle	possess. pron.	possessive pronoun
pref.	preface	p. adj.	participle adjective
prep.	preposition	pref.	prefix
pres. t.	present tense	pres. p.	present participle
pr. / pron.	pronoun	prop. n.	proper noun

Q

QA	Qatar	quot.	quotation

R

refl. / reflex.	Reflexive	reflex. pron.	reflexive pronoun

135

rel. pron.	relative pronoun	rh.	rhyming with
S			
Sat.	Saturday	Scand.	Scandinavian
Sept. Sep.	September	Shak.	Shakespeare
sing.	singular	SG	Singapore
ZA	South Africa	KR	Republic of *South Korea*
ES	Spain	spec.	specialized
spec. specif.	special specifically	subjunct.	subjunctive
sup. superl.	superlative	SE	Sweden
Sw.	Swedish	CH	Switzerland
sub. subj.	subject	Suf. / Suf.	Sufix
T			
TW	Taiwan	TH	Thailand
Th. / Thur	Thursday	trans.	transitive
transf.	Transfer transferred	transl.	translate translation
T. / Tue.	Tuesday	TR	Turkey
U			
AE	United Arab Emirates	GB	United Kingdom
US	United States	VN	Veitnam
V			
v.	verb	var.	variant
vbl. n.	verbal noun	verb. prefix	verbal prefix
verb. phr.	verbal phrase	v.r.	variant reading
W			
Wed.	Wednesday	W.	West, Wales, Welsh

❀ English Language Pronunciation Chart ❀

Table 53. International Phonetic Alphabet

Vowels							
Monophthongs				Diphthongs			
iː tr<u>ee</u> s<u>ea</u>t	ɪ s<u>i</u>t f<u>i</u>sh	ʊ g<u>oo</u>d p<u>u</u>t	uː f<u>oo</u>d sh<u>oe</u>	ɪə^r f<u>ea</u>r b<u>ee</u>r	eɪ <u>ei</u>ght th<u>ey</u>	—	
e b<u>e</u>t h<u>ea</u>d	ə <u>a</u>bout cin<u>e</u>ma	ɜːʳ g<u>ir</u>l l<u>ear</u>n	ɔː d<u>oo</u>r c<u>a</u>ll	ʊə t<u>ou</u>rist p<u>u</u>re	ɔɪ t<u>oy</u> ch<u>oi</u>ce	əʊ thr<u>ow</u> j<u>o</u>ke
æ <u>a</u>pple bl<u>a</u>ck	ʌ c<u>u</u>p l<u>o</u>ve	ɑː f<u>a</u>ther h<u>ear</u>t	ɒ st<u>o</u>p r<u>o</u>ck	eəʳ wh<u>ere</u> ch<u>air</u>	aɪ th<u>igh</u> <u>eye</u>	aʊ l<u>ou</u>nge c<u>ow</u>
Consonants							
p <u>a</u>pple <u>p</u>et	b a<u>b</u>out <u>b</u>ad	t <u>t</u>ime <u>t</u>ea	d <u>d</u>oor la<u>d</u>y	tʃ <u>ch</u>eck <u>ch</u>urch	dʒ lar<u>ge</u> loun<u>ge</u>	k wal<u>k</u> <u>c</u>at	g <u>g</u>reen fla<u>g</u>
f <u>f</u>ish <u>f</u>ood	v <u>v</u>oice fi<u>v</u>e	θ <u>th</u>ink ear<u>th</u>	ð <u>th</u>ey mo<u>th</u>er	s <u>s</u>top fa<u>s</u>t	z la<u>z</u>y noi<u>se</u>	ʃ <u>sh</u>oe cra<u>sh</u>	ʒ vi<u>si</u>on ca<u>s</u>ual
m <u>m</u>oney le<u>m</u>on	n <u>n</u>urse gree<u>n</u>	ŋ E<u>ng</u>lish si<u>ng</u>	h <u>h</u>ello <u>h</u>eart	l <u>l</u>ittle pu<u>ll</u>	r <u>r</u>ed t<u>r</u>ee	w <u>w</u>ind <u>w</u>et	j <u>y</u>ellow <u>y</u>ear

INDEX

A

abbreviations 133
abstract nouns 3, **6**, 13
academic writing 107
adjectives 3, 8, **17-23**, 27, 45, 68, 71, 74, 96, 109

  comparative and superlative **19-22**
  correct adjective order 22
  irregular 21
  meaning differences 22
  one-syllable **19-20**
  three or more syllables 21
  two-syllable **20-21**
  before nouns or after verbs 18

adverbs 18, 23, 48, 66, **68-74**, 76, 109

  amplifier 70
  degree **68**, 72, 74
  diminisher (tone down) 70
  emphasizer 70
  frequency **69**, 72
  manner 68, **69**, 72, 74
  place 66, 68, **69**, 72, 74
  placement 72
  time 68, **69**, 72, 74

adverb clause 89
adverb order 72
amplifier 70
apostrophe 2, 7, **99**

articles 1, **10-12**, 18, 19, 22
  definite 8, **11-12**
  general article rules 12
  indefinite 5, 9, **10-11**
  zero article rules **13-14**
  zero articles **12-14**
auxillary verbs 34-44

B

base verbs **32**, 35, 36, 38, 40, 45
bolding 105
brackets 99, **101**
bubble map 108, **110**
bullet points 106

C

capital letters **102**, 106
collective nouns 6
colon **93-94**, 106
comma 23, 73, 74, 81, 84, **88-93**, 100, 102
common nouns 4, 5, 6
comparative adjectives **19-22**
composition 107, 108, 110, **117**, 119
compound words 96
concluding sentences 112
concrete nouns 6

139

conjunctions	23, 66, **80-83**, 89, 91, 93, 109
coordinating	**80-81**, 89, 91
correlative and double	80, **82-83**, 109
subordinating	80, **81-82**, 83, 109
conjunctive adverbs	73-74
coordinating conjunctions	**80-81**, 89, 91
correct adjective order	22-23
correlative or double conjunctions	80, **82-83**, 109
contractions	99
count nouns	5
countable nouns	**5**, 6, 8, 9, 15, 64

D

dash	88, **95**, 100
date elements	91-92
definite article	8, **11-12**
demonstratives	1, 8, **14**, 18, 22
demonstrative pronouns	14, 26-27
acting like an adjective	27
determiners	1, **8-10**, 14, 16, 18, 22, 27
dialog text	90-91
dialogs and role-plays	121
diminisher (tone down)	70
down-toner (diminisher)	70
drafting	107, **110-114**, 118

E

editing	107, **118**
ellipsis	**87-88**, 90
emergence	139
emphasizer	70
empowerment	139
exclamation mark	84, 85, **86**, 87

H

harvard comma	89
homograph	114-117
homonym	114-117
homophone	114-117
hyphen	90, **96-98**

I

inconspicuous stressing	104-105
indefinite articles	5, 9, **10-11**
indefinite pronouns	30, 64, 65
interjections	**84**, 109
interrobang (interabang)	85, **87**
interrogative adverbs	74
interrogative pronouns	29-30
interruptions	90
introductory phrase	89
irregular adjectives	21
irregular verbs	**45**, 49
italics	104-105

140

M

main verbs **32**, 33, 34, 35, 36, 38, 39, 40, 41, 45, 47, 48, 49,

mass nouns 5

mind mapping 108-110

misused words 114-117

modal auxiliary verbs 34, 41-44

N

names 2, 4, 6, 13, **93**, 102, 103, 104

negative pronouns 31

non-descriptive adjectives 8

non-dialog text 90-91

nouns 1-7
  adding a suffix 3
  abstract 3, **6**, 13
  after a verb 1
  before and after a verb 1
  common 4, 5, 6
  concrete 6
  countable **5**, 6, 8, 9, 15, 64
  multi-syllable plural noun 2
  plural 4
  possessive 2, **7**, 8, **99**
  proper 2, **3**, 6, 94, 102, 106
  singular 4
  to express ownership 2
  to express the plural form 2
  uncountable **5,** 6, 8, 9, 15, 64

noun modifier 8

numbers 1, 8, 13, **16**, 22, 32, 86, 92, 93, 100, 115, 116, 178
  writing (spelt) numbers **96**

number elements 92

O

objective complement 18

omission of letters in a contraction 99

ordinals 1, 8, **16**, 22

organizing thoughts 107-108

oxford comma 89

P

paragraph construction 111-112

parentheses 88, **99-100**

parenthetical elements 88, 101

period (full stop) **85-86**, 87, 88, 94, 100, 102

personal pronouns **24-25**

places 3, 4, 13, **93**, 102

plural and singular nouns 4

possessive determiners 1, 8, **14**, 18, 19, 22, 25,

possessive nouns 2, **7**, 8, **99**

pre-determiner 16

prefix 97-98

prepositions 2, 24, 26, 29, 65, **75-79**, **96**, 103, 109, 130
  compound or complex 79
  place, space and direction
    (on, in, near, far) 77
  time (at, in, on, last, next, this) **78-79**

prewriting 107-110

141

primary aux. verbs	34, **35-41**
principal verbs	32
proactive monitoring	124
pronouns	14, 17, **24-31**
demonstrative	14, **26-27**
first, second, third-person	25
indefinite	30, 64, 65
interrogative	**29-30**
personal	**24-25**
reciprocal	31
relative	**28**, 29
proofing	107, **119**
proper nouns	2, **3**, 6, 94, 102, 106
publishing	58, 98. 107, **119-120**
punctuation	**85-106**, 109, 118

Q

quantifiers	1, 9, **15**, 18
question mark	85, **86-87**
quotation marks	86, 87, 90, **102**

R

reciprocal pronouns	31
regular verbs	45
relative pronouns	**28**, 29
revising	107, **118**
root word	**32**, 97, 98
rows and lines seating plan	129, **141**

S

semicolon	73, **94**

sentence unity and coherence	111, **112-114**
serial comma	89
series	49, **89**, 166
singular and plural nouns	4
spelt cardinals	96
spelt numbers	96
spider diagram	108, **109**
subject verb agreement	**64-67**
anyone, everyone, someone,	**64-65**
fractional expressions	66
neither and either	65
nor and or	66
nouns ending with 's'	**66-67**
positive vrs. negative subject	67
there and here	66
together with, as well as, along with	65
verbs in the present tense	66
submitting	107, **119**
subordinating conjunctions	80, **81-82**, 83, 109
suffix	98
superlative adjectives	**19-22**
supporting sentences	111-112
swung dash	95

T

terminating marks	**85-87**
exclamation mark	85, **86**
full stop (period)	**85-86**
interrobang (interabang)	85, **87**

question mark 85, **86-87**
period (full stop) **85-86**, 87, 88, 94, 100, 102
title 2, 3, 13, 86, 100, 102, 103, 104, 105, 108, 109
tone down (diminisher) 70
topic sentence **111**, 113
transitional sentence 110, **117-118**

U
---

uncountable nouns 5, 6, 8, 9, 15, 64
  the words *little* and *much* 5
  the words *some* and *any* 5
  voiced collectively 5

V
---

verbs 32-67
  active and passive voice 32-34
  auxiliary verb *'be'* and its forms 35-38
  auxiliary verb *'do'* and its forms 38-39
  auxiliary verb *'have'* and its forms 39-41
  base (main, principal, root) **32**, 35, 36, 38, 40, 45
  main (base, principal, root) **32**, 33, 34, 35, 36, 38, 39, 40, 41, 45, 47, 48, 49, 50
  modal auxillary 34, **41-44**
    can 42
    may and must 43
    shall, should, and ought (to) 43
    will 44
    would 44
  primary aux. (be, do, have) 35
  princilal 32
  regular and irregular 45
  tense and future time 46-63
    future continuous 54-55
    future perfect 59
    future perfect continuous 63
    future simple 50
    past continuous 52-53
    past perfect 58
    past perfect continuous 62
    past simple 49
    present continuous 51
    present perfect 56-57
    present perfect continuous 60-61
    present simple 47-48
  root (base, main, principal) **32**, 97, 98

W
---

words with a prefix 97-98
words with a suffix 98
writing guide 107-120

Z
---

zero articles 12-14
  general rules 13-14
zero determiners 12-14
  general rules 13-14

143

www.ingramcontent.com/pod-product-compliance
Lightning Source LLC
Chambersburg PA
CBHW070805100426
42742CB00012B/2249